DEALING WITH

THE IMPORTANCE OF MEDIA RELATIONS AND STRESS MANAGEMENT

CRITICAL INCIDENTS

FIRST EDITION

EDITED BY Robert Kirkland

Union Institute & University

cognella®
academic publishing

Bassim Hamadeh, CEO and Publisher
Kassie Graves, Director of Acquisitions
Jamie Giganti, Senior Managing Editor
Miguel Macias, Senior Graphic Designer
Mieka Porter, Senior Acquisitions Editor
Sean Adams, Project Editor
Luiz Ferreira, Senior Licensing Specialist
Kat Ragudos, Interior Designer

Cover image copyright © Depositphotos/slidezero.
        copyright © Depositphotos/woodstock.
        copyright © Depositphotos/robert_g.
        copyright © Depositphotos/zabelin.
        copyright © Depositphotos/s96serg.
        copyright © Depositphotos/DarioStudios.
        copyright © Depositphotos/photographee.eu.

Printed in the United States of America

ISBN: 978-1-63487-989-7 (pbk) / 978-1-63487-990-3 (br)

www.cognella.com   800-200-3908

Contents

Preface

C ritical Incident Management, as taught to law enforcement personnel, provides tactical direction designed to prevent, contain, manage, and resolve emergencies efficiently and effectively. Instructors, through their expertise, provide students with proven methodologies applicable to a host of scenarios that may be encountered in the public and private sectors.

In the Critical Incident Management course taught to Criminal Justice students at Union Institute and University, topics include: the phases of a critical incident response and stabilizing the scene; leadership style and techniques required to manage a critical incident successfully; media relations; guidelines for responding to hazardous materials and weapons of mass destruction incidents; stress management; maintaining continuity of business in the face of a crisis; and the roles of high-level personnel in setting policy and direction for the response and recovery efforts. Of all these topics, the two areas of most interest to students over the years have been media relations and stress management.

Critical Incidents are unplanned events such as natural disasters, hazardous materials spills, transportation disasters, workplace violence situations, and other life-threatening events. Consequently, an emergency response plan that provides the necessary structure for managing and effectively communicating during a critical incident is of vital importance to any organization. Besides helping to save lives and reduce property loss, a well-thought-out media response plan can serve to lessen an organization's potential liability.

In the realm of stress management, public safety personnel are exposed daily to a variety of potentially traumatic events, including human tragedies such as abused and distressed children, the aftermath of domestic violence, horrific motor vehicle accidents, disturbing crime scenes, disasters, and acts of terrorism. The importance of having Critical Incident Stress Management programs in place helps to mitigate the impact of these traumatic incidents on police officers and other emergency responders.

Indeed, both media relations and stress management are important areas to have mastered when a critical incident occurs. The most valuable resource in any organization is trained personnel. An organized and systematic approach to managing these two areas can go far in both keeping the public informed regarding a critical incident and maintaining the health and effective performance of law enforcement and emergency services personnel.

It is my hope that this text will further emphasize the importance of these two topics in law enforcement operations.

Dr. Robert Kirkland
Union Institute and University
robertkirklandconsulting.com

SECTION ONE

Media Relations during a Critical Incident

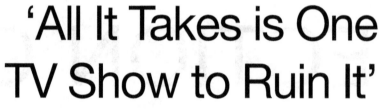

'All It Takes is One TV Show to Ruin It'

A Police Perspective on Police Media Relations in the Era of Expanding Prime Time Crime Markets

LAURA HUCY AND RYAN BROLL

I n this article, we draw on interviews conducted with Canadian police investigators for a study of mass media representations of police work to better understand their unique perspectives on the nature of police-media relations. In contrast to the orthodox position of the policing literature that holds that police are the dominant partner in the police-media relationship, investigators interviewed felt that they had lost control over representations of their work in media stories. This loss of control is attributed, in large part, to the pressure placed on reporters to feed an insatiable public appetite for

Laura Huey and Ryan Broll, "'All It Takes Is One TV Show to Ruin It': A Police Perspective on Police-Media Relations in the Era of Expanding Prime Time Crime Markets," *Policing & Society*, vol. 22, no. 4, pp. 384-396. Copyright © 2012 by Taylor & Francis Group. Reprinted with permission.

crime-related stories. Particularly, worrying for investigators is the belief that they are no longer able to maintain secrecy over their investigative activities and techniques—a shift that they see as having a significant negative impact on their work. What is required, officers believe, is better collaborative means of working with news media outlets.

Keywords: policing; news media

Introduction

In the latter half of the twentieth century, media representations of policing have become increasingly commonplace. These representations, which take the form of news accounts, fiction and a variety of entertainment-documentary hybrid programmes, have become a central feature of police organisational struggles for legitimacy (Reiner 2003). Perhaps not surprisingly, given both the importance and frequency of their representation by various forms of media, the police have become quite sensitive about their public image (Reiner 2003; Huey 2010). As Reiner explains, negative stories about police deviance are, not surprisingly, viewed with consternation. However, positive representations of policing also raise concerns, primarily that public expectations about their 'crime fighting wizardry or superhuman patience, tact, and integrity' will increase (Reiner 2003, p. 267; see also Huey 2010).

In this article, we draw on interviews conducted with police investigators for a study of mass media representations of police work to explore their unique perspectives on the nature of police-media relations. These investigators' experiences dealing with media outlets and/or seeing their work represented in print and television media stories lead many of those we studied to conclude that the public's insatiable appetite for crime-related stories has fundamentally altered the nature of police-media relations. With a twenty-four-hour news media increasingly driven to satisfy that appetite, police investigators feel that police organisations are no longer in control of their organisation's public image. Of particular concern for the majority of those interviewed, they also feel that police are no longer able to maintain secrecy over their investigative activities and techniques—a shift that they see as having a significant negative impact on their work.

To explore police perceptions concerning the nature of police-media relations in this era of expanding crime-related news coverage, we begin by examining the relevant literature on this relationship. The discussion then moves to an explanation of the methods used to acquire the data presented here and the techniques employed to analyse that data. We then examine police interviewee thoughts on their representation with news stories and, from there, to their concerns over the content of media messages about policing and the extent to which sensitive police information can be become public property. We then employ the example of a 'Mr. Big' operation, the details of which were publicly broadcast, to illustrate the organisational stresses that police feel can exist as a result of an ever-increasing public appetite for detailed policing stories. The discussion then shifts to what police have to say about how their organisations attempt to control how they are portrayed in news stories. Following this section, we turn to an analysis of the ways in which the police feel that they can and should work more effectively and cooperatively with news outlets to increase control over their representation in news stories. The article concludes with some final considerations on future research avenues.

The Complexity of Police-Media Relations

A considerable body of literature exists on the relationship between the police and the media, and the news management and public relations aspects of media management within police organisations (Chibnall 1977, 1979, Hall *et al.* 1978, Ericson *et al.* 1989, 1991, Schlesinger and Tumber 1994). Although the literature focuses on diverse aspects of the relationship, a number of key themes emerge which present what might be described as the orthodox view of the police-media relationship. To summarise this orthodoxy, scholars suggest that mass media images of policing are important, as they are a source of information on the police and on the whole have helped to legitimate police work. Conversely, the media also play an important 'watch-dog' role, acting on behalf of the general public to discover instances of police impropriety and miscarriages of justice. As a result of the latter, the police have generally been suspicious of their treatment by the media, despite the fact that content analysis studies have repudiated the basis of such suspicions (Chermack 1994). Regardless, this suspicion, which is often mutual, has contributed to a relationship between the police and the media which has been likened to a stormy marriage (Mawby 1999, p. 266). Within this stormy relationship, the police are frequently portrayed as the dominant partner. Indeed, within studies of policemedia relations the police are generally depicted as 'gatekeepers' to information sought by the media, gatekeepers who often recognise and exploit the media's need for exciting crime stories (Chibnall 1977, Hall *et al.* 1978, Ericson *et al.* 1989).

In describing police gatekeeping practices, researchers note that police agencies frequently withhold information from reporters (Ericson 1995). In fact, many police organisations have specific policies that require the exclusion of particular elements from discussions with the media. Most frequently, this includes denying information about victimisation, although in the past it was also generally understood that matters of police deployment and detection, police budgets, and internal priorities are not matters for the public record (Ericson *et al.* 1989). The most oft cited justification for such high levels of secrecy concerning police matters is that disclosures could jeopardise investigations and adversely influence the production and value of evidence. Another reason advanced by police agencies for secrecy over investigations is to maintain the privacy of civilians involved in a particular incident: victims, those considered vulnerable (e.g. youth), and those involved in sensitive matters (e.g. sexual offences) (Ericson *et al.* 1989). A less commonly discussed, but equally important, motive for withholding information from the media relates more directly to police operations. As Ericson *et al.* (1989, p. 128) explain, 'secrecy regarding police operational matters was [also] formulated in terms of not giving the criminal element information that would be to their benefit', such as specific investigative tactics that led to an arrest. Indeed, it is believed that any advantages associated with displaying one's investigative skills to the public would be overshadowed by the intelligence gained by potential criminals (Ericson *et al.* 1989, p. 128).

Nonetheless, in some instances the police will actively disclose knowledge of potential benefit to their operations and image (Ericson *et al.* 1989, Manning 2003). For example, they regularly seek out publicity related to specific law-enforcement crackdowns (e.g. drugs, gangs) based on the assumption that such publicity may have both a general deterrent effect and increase levels of public support (Ericson *et al.* 1989). Furthermore, the police often attempt to increase citizen consciousness about crime through major-occurrence news releases (Ericson *et al.* 1989) and to solicit the public's help when investigating high profile cases (Innes 2003). In such instances, however, if the police are unable to quickly solve the case the media attention they sought may backfire, and members of the media and the public may begin to question their competence (Innes 2003). Yet, another consideration is that involving the media in a case sometimes contributes to the high profile of a case, thus presenting an opportunity for an agency to secure additional funding and/or resources (Innes 2003). Given the increasing importance of publicity as an element of the police mandate (Ericson *et al.* 1989), in recent years some degree of cooperation with the news media has come to be seen as core components of police work and, as noted, has been included in many official policies (Ericson *et al.* 1989).

Returning briefly to the orthodox view discussed earlier—which suggests that the police hold a position of dominance in their relations with media—a growing body of literature suggests that a reappraisal of this perspective is required (Mawby 1999, Innes 2003). This reappraisal is required because police-media relations have grown increasingly complex, as have the institutions individually, making it ever more difficult for the police to manage the media (Mawby 1999). For example, the number of media outlets has expanded exponentially over the past few decades as we have entered an era of 24/7 news broadcasts, which has placed significantly more pressure on members of the media to develop stories. In turn, increased pressure is placed on the police to meet this growing demand (Mawby 1999). Thus, the days of an inner circle of reporters who are sympathetic to the police getting the scoop from friendly police officers in smoke filled bars are long gone (Ericson *et al.* 1989, Mawby 1999). A mutual understanding—wherein the police supplied information and the press portrayed the police favourably—has also long since disappeared, as both sides face increasing and often conflicting sets of institutional demands (Ericson *et al.* 1989). It is the effects of these pressures on police investigators' views of their treatment by mass media outlets that is the substantive focus of the present study.

Method of Inquiry

This article is informed by data drawn from in-depth qualitative interviews conducted with thirty-one Canadian police investigators for a study of the relationship of mass media production and police investigational work. The core concerns of this study were: (1) to determine to what extent media portrayals of police investigative work cohere with actual police roles and functions and (2) whether police investigators perceive media products as having an influence on public expectations in relation to their investigative role and work duties. The interview guide constructed in advance of entering the field contained a series of question related to the earlier research questions. It also included a series of questions related more generally to the relationship between mass media outlets and police organisations. Among questions posed to interviewees were variations of the following:

1. In what ways do police investigators and the organisations they work for attempt to control the representation of their work in media outlets?

2. How successful do they feel police are in controlling crime-related media messages?

3. What are the strengths and limitations of the strategies they employ to control the release of information to the media?

4. What are the perceived effects of media reporting on their work?

To answer these and other questions posed, approval to conduct interviews with police personnel was sought from municipal, regional and/or provincial police units from two Canadian provinces: British Columbia and Ontario. Seven police units representing two major Canadian cities and several medium-sized communities agreed to participate. Once this approval was secured, one of the authors conducted semi-structured interviews with police investigators from the following investigational units: homicide, major crimes, sexual assault, property crimes and forensic identification. Interviews typically ranged from one to two hours, with an average interview length of one and a half hours. Each interview was digitally recorded (Table 1.1).

To analyse the data collected, interview tapes were transcribed and then subjected to a two-stage coding process. In the first stage, open coding was used—that is, data were analysed thematically, with particular attention paid to how emergent themes addressed the research questions posed. To assist in the development of a list of appropriate notes were taken of potential themes during the interview process, with special attention paid to interviewees' choice of words in response to questions posed. In the second stage, focused coding was employed: transcripts were printed and then manually coded through line by line readings. To ensure reliability, as well as to identify emergent sub-themes, transcripts were reread and independently re-coded.

Table 1.1. Study participants.

Interviewee category	N
Police investigator	
Major crimes investigator	7
Homicide investigator	9
Sex crimes investigator	3
Property crimes investigator	1
Forensic identification officers	11
Total	31

How Police see their Representation in the Media

A recurring theme in interviews with police investigators was the desire to see police organisations exercise greater control over what information is released to the media and how this information is released. In large part, their views were borne from anger and/or dismay over what they saw as frequently erroneous depictions of themselves, their work or the operation of their organisation within media accounts. Indeed, one of the most frequently cited reasons for the development of these feelings was that news stories are often based on bits and pieces of 'evidence'; many officers felt that the media rarely presents the whole story. A Homicide Investigator explains in relation to investigative programmes such as *W5* in Canada and *60 Minutes* in the US, 'They never have all the information. They go on with bits and pieces'. Confounding this problem, he added, 'First and foremost, [the media usually present] a negative twist to the police investigation'. A Forensics Investigator echoes these sentiments: 'I've been to scenes and known the facts of what's going on and gone home and the news is completely off. They're broadcasting this stuff to be real and true and people are believing it'. A couple of respondents also believed that business interests may dictate which news stories are published or broadcast. For example, the Property Crimes Investigator interviewed—a self-proclaimed news junkie—explained that the media 'form their opinions, their views, their values on what they want to do and sell it to make money. You know, the media will say what they want to say… Sexy, flashy, glamorous—that's what they want. High impact stories!'

Of greater concern to interviewees, however, are those instances when they do cooperate with the media, only to find that they have been misquoted or misrepresented in the resulting news story. Respondents frequently noted this as being an especially egregious problem that significantly and negatively influences their relationships with members of the media. A Major Crimes Investigator, for example, stated: 'I've never seen media stories—including of my own testimony—that were ever accurate'. A Homicide Investigator similarly noted: 'I've been in court and given evidence and I've read the paper the next day and they've described me in court and what I said, and I've sat back and thought, "That's not the same court case I was in"'. A Major Crimes Investigator stated: 'I have had instances where I was interviewed for five minutes and they take two excerpts from different segments and put them together and it's not at all the way it was said'.

As a response, some interviewees stated that they no longer follow the news media. Others explained that they and their fellow officers read or watch the news, but joke about what the 'real story is'. As one police officer stated, few police investigators treat the news as gospel. Still others noted that misrepresentations of their work in media stories often draw unfair criticism from both media and the general public. Given the extent to which interviewees reported instances of misrepresentation in the media, it is perhaps not surprising that the majority of interviewees held particularly strong opinions regarding news outlets' portrayal of their work. For instance, several reported feeling disrespected by the media, believing that they are only portrayed as 'knuckle-dragging donut-eaters'. A Homicide

Investigator succinctly conveyed this position by noting, 'I actually can't remember ever reading an article where they talked about how nice an investigator was or how professional they were or how dedicated they were'. A Homicide Investigator from another organisation concurs: 'Just look at the newspaper. Either we're heroes and brilliant or we're complete idiots, and there's very little in between'.

While some officers were clearly resentful about negative portrayals and what was often perceived to be unfair criticism, others viewed it as simply a part of the job. Indeed, one officer stated that he 'learned to let it be like water of a duck's back'. Those who echoed this latter perspective stated that regardless of their representation in the media, they still have a job to do and cannot let media stories affect their work. This point is represented within the following quotation from an interview with a Homicide Investigator:

> No matter what the police do, there's a voice saying 'You shouldn't have done that,' or 'You should have done that.' Do I think it plays a role in or impacts our job? I don't think it does because no matter what they show on TV, or no matter what they portray the police as, the day-to-day policeman has a job to do and there are only certain ways you can do it.

Of particular concern for several interviewees is the speed at which members of the media are forced to operate. Clearly, the police and the media have competing demands: while the media timeframe relates to print and on-air deadlines, the police timeframe relates to the gathering of evidence that will lead to a conviction in court. Consequently, as a Major Crimes Investigator commented, members of the media generally do not 'like the pace that we go at in order to get the evidence that will stick in court'. The quicker pace at which members of the media must work to meet deadlines, often raises concerns that the media will compromise an investigation. The same investigator also noted observing instances when members of the media approached key witnesses for stories. One of the authors observed the effects of this dynamic while conducting interviews for this study in a homicide unit. During this time, a high profile case involving the murder of a young professional woman was a major media event. To generate newsworthy information and comments to fill out their stories, reporters were interviewing the woman's family, friends and neighbours. Several of the resulting stories featured headlines suggesting that police had identified the woman's husband as their prime suspect and that an arrest would be imminent. While decrying the fact that reporters were 'trampling on their investigation', knocking on doors to talk to potential police witnesses, the head of the homicide unit told the author in a somewhat aggrieved tone, 'the media says that the husband's our suspect, and *I* don't even know if he's our suspect'.

Too Much Information is Getting Out

A common theme to emerge in interviews was that media outlets—drawing on information gleaned through 'trampling an investigation'—release too much information to the public that police would like withheld. In fact, all those interviewed were of the view that too much information is being released about policing and investigative tactics, and that these disclosures are problematic for police.

The most frequently cited reason for withholding information from the public was to maintain the integrity of the investigation. Respondents indicated concern that making certain facts public may jeopardise the investigation in both the short term (e.g. gathering evidence, interviewing witnesses) and the long term (e.g. if the case goes to trial, possible parole hearings in the future). As the Property Crimes Investigator explained:

> the media does not realize that at, the end of the day, you're really hurting not only the investigation but you're probably hurting thousands or hundreds more because there's a certain technique that the police have used for many years that has worked, that has been proven credible, but now you're all of a sudden making the decision to now let the public know exactly what's going on. You know, the police will have to come up with something new.

In relation to questions about the types of information that, when released, can be harmful to an investigation, several interviewees expressed concerns that photo line-ups can be compromised as a result of the publicising of suspects in news stories. As a Homicide Investigator explained, the media 'shows photographs of the suspect, which means that we can no longer run photo line-ups with our witnesses because they've already seen the person on television'. A Homicide Investigator from another police department recounted an example from a recent case he worked on:

> A: One girlfriend phones the suspect and says, 'You wouldn't believe what I just saw on TV. I don't think you and your friends are who they say they are.' And that's where that type of information is being published in the media, that's where it's going—it's reaching these targets that we're working on.

> Q: And that becomes quite problematic.

> A: Yes, and expensive for us as we invest all this time and effort into these techniques and all it takes is one TV show to ruin it.

Of particular concern to interviewees was the fact that an infinite number of investigative techniques are not available, and that investigations might suffer as a result of too much information about police trade craft being leaked to the public. When asked for an example of a media story that depicted the extent to which police investigators felt they had lost the ability to control the type and/or amount of information released by media outlets, interviewees had several instances to draw from. The examples provided ranged from news stories about police deaths in custody, to a high profile pepper spray incident, to a media broadcast of the details of a police undercover operation. Of these, in this section we want to specifically look at the latter: the Mr. Big Case.[1]

In 2007, an American broadcaster released a prime time 'true crime' news show on the subject of a Canadian police investigation into a high profile murder case. Within the hour long programme, detailed information was provided with respect to how the police lured the suspects into confessing through the use of an undercover agent—a classic police set-up known as a 'Mr. Big' operation.

One of the authors interviewed a police investigator who had worked on the case and was significantly upset about the level of information that the broadcaster had been able to secure—through a court-ordered subpoena of files related to the case—and subsequently made public. When asked about the source of his unhappiness, he stated that the release of information concerning police operational techniques, such as Mr. Big, 'compromises the technique. That technique solves an awful lot of murders. More than any forensic case ever will!'. An investigator in another department with knowledge of both the case and the television programme noted of the broadcast: 'They put a lot of detail on the scene, a lot of detail on the investigation and I think worst, a lot of detail on the undercover technique'. Similarly another colleague stated: 'It pretty much gave up the whole Mr. Big scenario and how it worked'. A Major Crimes Investigator in another unit opined about the television programme, 'that should not have been released, that's a technique—a trade craft, you could say—a police trade craft that should not be disclosed to the public'. The head of an investigative unit, also with knowledge of the case, was asked whether he was surprised by the amount of detailed information that was made public. His reply:

> I wouldn't say stunned. Probably, of course, because I knew that was coming. It had been delayed from an earlier time. If it had been broadcast at that earlier date, there would have been more of a shock value to investigators, although there certainly was shock value to people in the investigative field that that would come out. But [information about police techniques are] coming out more and more and more in the papers.

One of the concerns frequently raised by media outlets in defense of releasing information about police activities is that such information can be of important public interest pertaining to issues of civilian oversight. An experienced police investigator was asked whether there was a public interest component that would justify release of details concerning the police use of this technique. His response: 'No, I don't think so'. In subsequent interviews with police members of both this same organisation and others—all of whom had at least passing knowledge of the case, the technique and the television broadcast—this view was widely shared.

Trying to Control the Message

In each of the interviews conducted, respondents were asked about the extent to which they or their organisation attempt to control the message that is portrayed by the media, about both specific cases and policing more generally. Given that most individuals interviewed felt police had generally lost control over how they are portrayed in mass media, it is of little surprise that the majority of respondents were of the view that it is important to control information presented to the general public and that their organisation could do more to alter misconceptions fuelled by media stories.

In relation to what their organisations currently do to control the flow of information, several interviewees identified prepared media releases as being the way in which the police are able to exercise the greatest control. Media releases permit extensive control in at least two ways: first, the police are able to carefully select and edit the words and details included, and second, individual officers in an investigation do not have to immediately respond to media questions probing for more information.

Another primary means by which police organisations seek to control media accounts of their work is through the use of designated media relations officers (MROs), who prepare press releases, field media calls and represent the police organisation at press conferences and media events. The use of MROs thus serves to take pressure off investigators. As a Major Crimes Investigator explained, referring requests to the MRO serves the dual purpose of having specially trained representatives relaying the police message and interacting with the media, but it also helps to relieve investigators of what are often viewed as unwanted distractions. Similarly, the Property Crimes Investigator exclaimed that by referring requests to the MRO, 'I get to wash my hands of it pretty quick'. However, some problems do arise from an extensive reliance on MROs. For example, if important messages need to be made public, a Major Crimes Investigator noted that a lack of resources in the Media Relations department 'often delays the message getting out because there's only one or two people doing that'.

Despite some recognised limitations, most interviewees felt that the benefits of having a dedicated MRO far outweigh the pitfalls. Several officers stated they believe that when a small group of officers have regular contact with the media, the police are better able to present their message and effectively control what is revealed to the public. Importantly, MROs are able to learn who can be trusted, and who within the media they must handle with caution. One Homicide Investigator was herself a former media relations officer. In discussing MRO work, she explained: 'you could filter and protect what would get out. They could still misquote me and take it where they wanted to take it anyway, but you could learn which [members of the] media you could talk to and which [members of the] media you would get along with'. If she was misquoted too often, information would no longer be provided to that journalist. In this sense, the orthodox view of the relationship—wherein the police occupy the more dominant position vis-a-vis the media—may hold.

The Need to Rethink Media Strategy

While recognising the importance of attempting to control both the release of information and the representation of the police agency and its workers, the majority of those interviewed were also cognizant of the fact that trying to control the message too much can have negative consequences, as it pushes media outlets into seeking other sources to develop their stories. Furthermore, failing to provide information to the public in a timely fashion can raise suspicions about police actions. For example, a Homicide Investigator argued that providing detailed accounts of an investigation to the public immediately may assist in removing some suspicion of police actions, especially in relation to incidents wherein a member of the public is injured. Referencing a high-profile case in which a suspect was killed while in police custody, a Major Crimes Investigator concurred:

> It is extremely frustrating for police. We all wanted our media liaison people to get on the air and put the other side of the shoe forwards. I certainly wished there was more proactive work done by our side to explain the investigation...
> I think we want to control the message a bit too much. It may be helpful for the public if they heard from the grassroots member without rehearsing or anything like that.

Indeed, controlling the message too much or withholding too much information may raise curiosity or suspicion among members of the public. Several respondents recognised that this often leads members of the public to wonder what the police are hiding. This point was clearly articulated by a Property Crimes Investigator, who commented, 'We always say "no comment" or "we can't say anything about that right now because we're still investigating", etcetera... When we say stuff like that the public automatically jumps on, and the media immediately jumps on, 'what are they hiding?''.

Not only does offering 'no comment' raise suspicion, but it also forces the media to use alternative sources to gather their information. For investigators, this can be especially problematic and may lead to the levels of misinformation that they perceive to exist in the news media. To prevent such things from happening, a Major Crimes Investigator explained that media relations courses currently being offered through his organisation teach officers not to give too much information to the media, but also not to 'shut down' reporters altogether. Offering too little information, he suggested, leads the media to contact members of the public—including neighbours and family members of the victim or the accused—to develop their stories, with the potential that an investigation might be harmed, as witnesses are potentially compromised.

In response to perceived problems with the media representation of policing, police officers and various policing techniques, the majority of interviewees indicated a need for police agencies to work more effectively and cooperatively with media outlets to frame policing messages in more positive ways. One of the most frequently identified methods for doing so was to use news outlets as a tool to better educate the public on the police mandate and role. For example, a Homicide Investigator noted that:

> one of the things that we've undertaken here is to start educating the public within these [media] releases about what we can and cannot do. That we don't make the laws; that the case law is driven by the courts and we have to abide by those. That we don't lay the charges; we build the case and put it forward, but we don't lay the charges.

Alongside press releases, taking more time to talk to those reporters covering investigations, to explain necessary processes, was thought to be a beneficial approach. A Sex Crimes Investigator explained, for instance, that people are often quite receptive when he explains the differences between media representations of his work and the realities of policing to them. A Homicide Investigator clearly articulates this vision when he said: 'I would just like to raise the bar in terms of how we provide information to the media, the public, and how the media reports it. So much of it just looks like we're just trying to protect ourselves from criticism rather than genuinely educating people'. This view was shared by other police officers, who similarly thought that the most effective method of educating the media, and thus the public, was to be both more forthright and forthcoming. For example, a Property Crimes Investigator advocated for greater transparency as follows: 'Rather than saying "no comment", give a little of the obvious about it. And that's all people need, a little bit of the obvious. For us to say, "This is where we're at, this is what we're doing, and this is what we hope to do", and I think we could do a better job at that'. He went on to propose that seeking outside help, from retired members of the media, for example, in training officers in media relations may be a valuable and necessary step in articulating their message more effectively.

Several investigators interviewed explained that working harder to develop collaborative relations with the media would be especially useful in helping the police regain a measure of the control they felt they had lost. A Major Crimes investigator developed this idea further by explaining that 'instead of the two factions (the police and the media) going, 'What are they going to say, what are they going to do', we [need to] develop more of a relationship, a business relationship with the media'. He felt that developing these relationships may increase trust and may result in the media presenting fewer stories based on speculation since the journalist would know the subject of the story personally. Such a self-reinforcing and mutually beneficial relationship would not only allow the police to take some control back and alleviate some concerns over unethical reporting practices, but it would also provide members of the media with their much needed access to police officers and copy material.

Concluding Remarks

To recall, the orthodox view of police-media relations suggests that the police occupy a dominant position in the relationship, while the media serves an important purpose by providing an element of civilian oversight (Chermack 1994). In contrast to the orthodox view, however, some have suggested that a minimal level of cooperation with the media has become an important component of police work (Ericson *et al.* 1989) and a growing body of literature argues that a complete reappraisal of the orthodox view is necessary (Mawby 1999, Innes 2003). According to this latter perspective, increasingly complex relations between the police and the media have qualitatively altered the nature of the association and have made it ever more difficult for the police to control the media (Mawby 1999, Innes 2003).

Although the police may occupy a position of dominance on select occasions—such as when MROs discontinue cooperation with members of the media who frequently misquote them—our findings suggest that police officers interviewed perceive the media as occupying a more dominant position, and some feel that they have lost control over their representation in media stories. Given the rapid expansion of prime time crime markets and the exponential increase in the number of media outlets, there was also awareness among interviewees that it was imperative that they develop new strategies and tactics for more effectively dealing with the media. Consequently, there is an explicit desire among officers to work more cooperatively with the media in ways that may prove to be beneficial for the police, including using the media as a tool through which to educate the public on the police role, function and mandate. Such strategies must be developed with full awareness of the fact that the police must consider both the short-term and long-term implications of making certain information public, thus there will always be a need to negotiate precariously between the public's right to know and operational requirements for secrecy.

Notwithstanding the aforementioned conclusions, three noteworthy limitations of this study must be addressed. First, interviews were conducted with officers from two major Canadian cities and several medium-sized cities. It is possible—and perhaps likely—that these urban centres differ in meaningful ways from other regions. Certainly, the extent of the media presence in these cities differs markedly from that of smaller cities and towns in Canada and other countries. Second, most of those interviewed were senior ranking officers with several years of investigational experience. It is possible that experience is an important factor in structuring one's relationship with members of the media, as well as one's perceptions. Finally, although one officer interviewed had previously served as a MRO we did not directly recruit MROs for this study. Given their more frequent contract with the media, it is possible that MROs perspectives may differ from those of detectives and other police investigators.

While the present article offers an useful contribution to the literature in this field, there remains a continuing need for further research that focuses on the evolving nature of the relationship between the police and the media. Indeed, more diverse samples of policing agencies may provide unique comparative insights into the dynamics of the relationship in urban centres compared to more rural areas. Moreover, cross-national comparisons of the relationship may shed further insights. For example, we still now far too little about the extent to which the police-media relationship in Canada and the US (which have comparable media outlets and policing structures) is similar to or differ from that in the

UK, Australia and elsewhere. Finally, a greater emphasis should be placed on understanding the media's perception on their relationship with the police, as much of the research to date provides one side of the story—that of the police. Members of the media may have a qualitatively different understanding of their interactions with the police.

Note

1. To protect the identities of those who participated in this study, we are deliberately choosing to leave out some of the identifying details of this case, as well as similarly identifying information concerning the subsequent broadcast of this case on a major American news network.

References

Chermack, S., 1994. Crime in the news media: a refined understanding of how crimes become news. *In:* G. Barak, ed. *Media, process, and the social construction of crime.* New York: Garland Publishing, 95–130.

Chibnall, S., 1977. *Law-and-order news: an analysis of crime reporting in the British press.* London: Tavistock Publications.

Chibnall, S., 1979. The metropolitan police and the news media. *In:* S. Holdaway, ed. *The British police.* London: Edward Arnold, 135–149.

Ericson, R.V., 1995. *Crime and the media.* Aldershot: Dartmouth.

Ericson, R., Baranek, P., and Chan, J., 1989. *Negotiating control: a study of news sources.* Toronto: University of Toronto Press.

Ericson, R., Baranek, P., and Chan, J., 1991. *Representing order: crime, law, and justice in the news media.* Toronto: University of Toronto Press.

Hall, S., *et al,* 1978. *Policing the crisis.* London: Macmillan.

Huey, L., 2010. 'I've seen this on CSI': criminal investigators and the management of public expectations in the field. *Crime, Media, Culture,* 61 (1), 49–68.

Innes, M., 2003. *Investigating murder: detective work and the police response to criminal homicide.* Oxford: Clarendon Press.

Manning, P., 2003. *Policing contingencies.* Chicago: University of Chicago Press.

Mawby, R., 1999. Visibility, transparency and police media relations. *Policing and Society,* 9 (2), 263–286.

Reiner, R., 2003. Policing and the media. *In:* T. Newburn, ed. *Handbook of policing.* Cullompton: Willan, 259–281.

Schlesinger, P. and Tumber, H., 1994. *Reporting crime: the media politics of criminal justice.* Oxford: Oxford University Press.

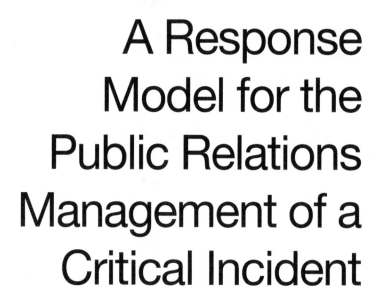

A Response Model for the Public Relations Management of a Critical Incident

DAVID GILLINGHAM AND JEREMIE NOIZET

Introduction

The organisational response to a critical incident can have a major impact on how the organisation is perceived in both the short and long term. The effective management of public relations during and after an incident can lead to major organisational benefits. This paper proposes a four-element model (see list below) for how organisations should manage their public relations when they are faced with a critical incident.

David Gillingham and Jeremie Noizet, "A Response Model for the Public Relations Management of a Critical Incident," *Disaster Prevention and Management*, vol. 16, no. 4, pp. 545-550. Copyright © 2007 by Emerald Group Publishing Limited. Reprinted with permission.

The paper then uses five short case studies to illustrate how the four elements contribute to the successful management of real incidents. The four-element model is as follows:

1. *Think of the public and the media:*
   » understand their concerns; and
   » start from the public's point-of-view.

2. *Act fast:*
   » be the first to talk;
   » control the message;
   » get to the scene; and
   » take action.

3. *Be straight:*
   » be honest;
   » be consistent;
   » be clear; and
   » use corporate values.

4. *Show concern and compassion:*
   » show that people and the environment come first;
   » be human; and
   » be involved.

The Four Elements of the Model

THINK OF THE PUBLIC AND THE MEDIA

At the moment that an incident takes place the organisation needs to think about this crisis from the point-of-view of the public and the media. The organisation needs to base its communications on the perceptions of the public and not on its own understanding of the event. If the external world thinks there is a problem then there is a problem (Bierck, 2000). The public needs to comprehend the crisis and understand how it might affect them (Coombs, 1999). Implicit communications are very important to the public and the media as they indicate the veracity of the source. Hence, it is important to be well prepared and to be self-confident (Bierck, 2000).

In no circumstances should an organisation respond to an incident by saying it has no comment. This will be interpreted negatively and will hand control of the communications over to the media.

ACT FAST

The stakeholders involved need to be informed about the incident within a matter of hours (Orgizek and Guillery, 1999). The media needs to be made aware of the situation rapidly and if the organisation does not talk then the information will come from another source (Harrison, 2000). If information is not available immediately then this leaves room for speculative stories by the media (Ashcroft, 1997). It is vital to keep control of the information (Ogrizek and Guillery, 1999) and failure to do so gives an impression that the organisation does not know what is happening (Harrison, 2000).

There is a need for extensive communication in the first few days of the crisis (Bierck, 2000) and an organisation often establishes its authority in a crisis by being the first to talk wisely about the situation (Harrison, 2000). If an organisation cannot respond rapidly with genuine information then it will be judged negatively.

The organisation needs to communicate what it is doing about the incident and how well it is caring for people and looking after the environment (Bierck, 2000). The involvement of senior management at an early stage is critical (McHenry, 1996) and the direct involvement of the CEO is often crucial to the successful management of the situation. The Chief Executive's involvement at press conferences and at the incident scene adds weight and credibility to the communication (Bierck, 2000). The CEO is then seen to take personal responsibility and is perceived to be more likely to tell the truth.

The communications messages need to be agreed and understood by all those involved and the appointment of a single spokesperson helps to maintain a consistent message. It is important to communicate with all stakeholders, including the organisation's employees. The tone of the message also needs to be adjusted to fit the incident.

BE STRAIGHT

The organisation needs to tell the truth (Ashcroft, 1997; Harrison, 2000) and denying can be very damaging (Coombs, 1999). The organisation needs to make its plan for solving the problem public and to make them clearly understood by using clear and simple language (McHenry, 1996). Transparency is essential and there should be clear signs that the organisation takes the matter very seriously and that investigations will be undertaken (Bierck, 2000). In responding to incidents organisations should reflect their own positive values (Ogrizek and Guillery, 1999).

If the organisation knows that it is at fault then it is best to admit it and show concern. It is much worse to deny the truth and for it to emerge at a later date.

SHOW CONCERN AND COMPASSION

Organisations need to be seen to be warm and human not cold and calculating. They need to express sorrow quickly after the incident and to express understanding and sympathy for the victims (Harrison, 2000). The company's initial behaviour towards the victims sets the tone for all subsequent situations. It is essential to show commitment to victims and to providing assistance (Ogrizek and Guillery, 1999). The organisation should apologise promptly when appropriate (Ashcroft, 1997). Often the organisation needs to resist the efforts of lawyers and insurers in order to express compassion and provide assistance (Black, 1993; Harrison, 2000). Expressing concern does not mean that the organisation accepts responsibility and compassion is always appropriate since it shows that caring is its highest priority (Coombs, 1999). On the contrary denial shows lack of care and is seen to be not compassionate. Organisations should always act ethically in a crisis and show that they care about people, safety and the victims (Bierck, 2000).

Case Vignettes

PERRIER

Perrier is the manufacturer of a well-known sparkling mineral water. On February 7 1990 management were informed that traces of Benzene had been found in 13 bottles of water in the USA. On February 9 Perrier withdrew all bottles from sale in the USA. Meanwhile traces were also found in France. On February 14 Perrier withdrew all bottles worldwide although experts agreed that there was a negligible health risk.

At first Perrier seemed unprepared for such an incident and different messages were communicated in different markets. However, Perrier rapidly withdrew the product and launched a communications strategy based on safety first. Empty shelf space in retailers was used to explain its safety first approach and to advertise the re-launch of the product. There was little media criticism of Perrier.

COCA-COLA DASANI WATER

Coca-Cola is one of the world's largest soft drinks manufacturers. Dasani is treated bottled tap water, which is well established in the USA as the leading brand. In January 2004 Coca-Cola launched Dasani in the UK. In March several British newspapers mocked Coca-Cola for selling tap water in bottles. On March 19 there were reports that Dasani contained twice the UK legal limit of bromate, a chemical which may cause cancer. The first Coca-Cola press release announced the voluntary withdrawal of 500,000 bottles of Dasani in the UK. The company postponed the launch of Dasani in France and Germany. Subsequent press coverage was highly critical of Coca-Cola's public relations and the marketing fiasco. The company was perceived to have tried to deceive the public by marketing public water supplies as pure still water akin to water from natural sources.

TOTALFINA-ERIKA

The inspections of the Erika by Maritime Authorities in several different countries revealed a history of problems from 1996. In November 1999 she passed an inspection by the Italian regulators. On December 11 the Erika was caught in a severe storm and started to take on water. On December 12 the crew was evacuated by helicopter as the ship started to break-up off the French coast. Ten days after the incident the CEO of TotalFina made the first declaration that the company was willing to participate in compensation and coastline cleaning but that whilst the company was concerned it was not guilty as it was chartering the ship. This slow response was seen to be a sign of an uncaring company and the CEO was highly criticised. On December 30 TotalFina issued its first press release which covered its involvement with the authorities, its plans to address the problems and its plans to restore the environment. In its second press release on January 14 2000 the company expressed its concerns and its commitment to improve maritime safety but once again said it was not responsible.

The communications by TotalFina were seen as attempts by the company to avoid responsibility. They were not sufficiently compassionate about damage to the fishing industry and to the coastline. No one from TotalFina visited the coastline and the company mishandled the press. The Sea Accidents Investigation Office found that the Erika broke apart most likely because of a structural weakness. The Erika was an old ship without a double-hull.

After the incident TotalFina continued to make mistakes and were criticised by the press, politicians and environmentalists.

SHELL-IEVOLI SUN

The Ievoli Sun was chartered by Shell and had recently passed an inspection by the Italian Maritime Authority. On October 29, 2000 the Ievoli Sun, carrying 6,000 tons of chemicals—including styrene, was caught in a violent storm in the English Channel. On October 30 her crew was evacuated by helicopter as she had structural damage to her double-hull. Whilst being towed towards the French coast the ship sank near the Island of Alderney. On the same day Shell and Exxon Mobil both issued a press release announcing that they would offer every possible assistance to the authorities. On November 1 the chairman of Shell France headed a team of experts who went to Alderney. The company issued a second press release announcing its continued assistance and a spokesperson acknowledged the dangers to marine life. He also stated that Shell would do all that it could to help and that the company had drawn up contingency plans. The situation was seen to be under control. By the end of June Shell, together with the French and British Authorities, had completed the clean-up operations as suggested by Shell. There was no apparent pollution by dangerous chemicals. The media coverage was reasonably positive and initial concerns had passed as Shell was seen to be taking responsibility and caring about what happened.

AIR FRANCE AND ADP, TERMINAL 2E

In June 2003 Terminal 2E at Charles de Gaulle Airport was opened as a new hub for Air France international flights. The airport is operated by Aeroports de Paris (ADP). On May 22 2004 police noticed a crack in the wall of the terminal, photographs were taken but no further action was taken. On May 23 more cracks appeared and police began evacuations but 12 minutes later, at 7.57 am, a section of the roof collapsed killing six people. Air France released a press release that afternoon expressing its compassion, offering support to the victim's families and announcing ADP's care line telephone number. The Chairman of Air France visited the scene of the accident the same day. ADP issued its own press release expressing compassion for the victims families. On May 24 the President of ADP announced that the whole terminal would be demolished if the other sections appeared to be unsound. He said ADP would take no risk when it came to safety. This counteracted a rumour that Air France and ADP had put pressure on the contractors to complete the building. The architect who designed Terminal 2E flew back from China to assist the investigation.

The President of ADP announced that his two principles were respect for the victims and transparency. ADP organised a remembrance service at the Airport and gave financial compensation before there were any insurance reports. In August the terminal was partially reopened after the structure had been reinforced.

On balance the press coverage was reasonably positive because of the rapid response by the companies and their evident compassion and transparency.

Lessons From the Case Studies

THINKING OF THE PUBLIC AND THE MEDIA

Initially, Perrier was confused, however it quickly understood the concerns of the public and the media. Coca-Cola did not seem to understand public concerns and was perceived to have tried to deceive the public. TotalFina certainly did not start from looking at the incident from the public's point-of-view. Its lack of response and apparent lack of concern was at odds with the public interest. Shell seems to have well understood the likely concerns and acted accordingly. Similarly, Air France and ADP seemed to be particularly good at thinking about the incident from the point-of-view of the victims.

ACT FAST

Perrier took time to react and started out with a confused message. However, once it understood then it took firm control of both the action and the message. Coca-Cola never seemed to be in control of the message with the result that it was mocked by the press. TotalFina acted very slowly with the result that the media were in control of the message and the company became a scapegoat criticised by the media, politicians and environmentalists. Shell took very rapid action, it was the first to talk to the media, it was quickly on the scene, it took firm action and was in control of the message. Air France and ADP responded extremely rapidly with appropriate messages delivered from the scene of the accident. They took firm and decisive action.

BE STRAIGHT

Perrier was honest with the public and after initial confusion it was consistent and clear. Coca-Cola was perceived to be deceiving the public and whilst it took quick action it was nevertheless seen to be unclear and unethical. TotalFina was seen to be trying to get away from any responsibility. Shell was seen to be honest, with consistent and clear communications about the incident and its plans for tackling the situation. Air France and ADP were seen to be honest, consistent and clear in their communications.

SHOW CONCERN AND COMPASSION

Perrier was seen to be concerned about the problem and to have taken firm and decisive action worldwide. Coca-Cola was seen as being concerned about bromate but unconcerned about deceiving consumers about the origin of the water in Dasani. TotalFina was seen as being unconcerned and lacking in compassion about the livelihoods of the fishing communities and damage to the environment. It became a company that many people in France used as a negative symbol of the race for profit, both inhuman and unethical. Shell was seen as both concerned and compassionate, keen to protect the environment with human involvement at the highest levels. Air France and ADP were exemplary in their compassionate approach to the victims and their families. They quickly involved their most senior people in press statements.

Conclusions

Those companies that effectively used the four elements of the public relations process appear to have gained not only from the short term benefits of improved management of the incidents involved but also from a long-term effect on their corporate reputations. Perrier, Shell, Air France and ADP all seem to enjoy good reputations whilst Coca-Cola still seems to suffer from the Dasani disaster and TotalFina is still seen rather negatively, especially in France.

References

Ashcroft, L.S. (1997), "Crisis management—public relations", *Journal of Managerial Psychology,* Vol. 12 No. 5, pp. 325–32.

Bierck, R. (2000), "How to handle a media crisis", *Harvard Management Communication Letter,* Vol. 3 No. 3.

Black, S. (1993), *The Essentials of Public Relations,* Kogan Page, London.

Coombs, W.T. (1999), "Information and compassion in crisis responses: a test of their effects", *Journal of Public Relations Research,* Vol. 11 No. 2, pp. 125–42.

Harrison, S. (2000), *Public Relations: An Introduction,* Thomson Learning, Padstow.

McHenry, J. (1996), "Panic free PR crisis management", *Marketing Computers,* Vol. 16 No. 2, pp. 26–7.

Ogrizek, M. and Guillery, J-M. (1999), *Communicating in Crisis,* Walter de Gruyter, New York, NY.

Police-Media Relations at Critical Incidents
Interviews from Oklahoma City

TORY J. CAETI, JOHN LIEDERBACH
AND STEVEN S. BELLEW

Tory Caeti PhD is currently an Assistant Professor in the Department of Criminal Justice at the University of North Texas. He has authored or coauthored over 20 journal articles, books and manuscripts, and his articles have appeared in Crime and Delinquency, Law and Policy, American Journal of Criminal Law, and Criminal Justice Policy Review. In addition, he has been awarded research grants to study topics including law enforcement and victim services, saturation patrol methodologies, juvenile homicide trends, and drugs and crime. His current research interests include police patrol, administration and management, crime

Tory J. Caeti, John Liederbach, and Steven S. Bellew, "Police-Media Relations at Critical Incidents: Interviews from Oklahoma City," *International Journal of Police Science & Management*, vol. 7, no. 2, pp. 86-97. Copyright © 2005 by SAGE Publications. Reprinted with permission.

analysis, and criminal justice policy. John Liederbach PhD is currently an Assistant Professor in the Department of Criminal Justice at the University of North Texas. His research interests include police work load analysis, small-town and rural policing, and white-collar and professional crime. His work has appeared in Justice Quarterly, American Journal of Criminal Justice, and Police Forum.

Steven S. Bellew has an MSc in Criminal Justice from the University of North Texas. He is employed by the Federal Protective Service.

Abstract

The policing of critical incident scenes, including natural disasters, hazardous materials spills, hostage situations, and terrorist attacks, has become an especially salient topic in the post-September 11 environment. Given the attention-grabbing nature of these events, police administrators are often faced with the task of building and maintaining relationships with members of the media at these scenes, primarily reporters and their crews who often pursue goals that are in direct conflict with those of law enforcement. This article examines the issues related to police-media relations at critical incident scenes using interview data from subjects involved in policing the scene of the Oklahoma City bombing and the related trials of Timothy McVeigh and Terry Nichols. These interviews provide a context for the presentation of guidelines important to police administrators who must be able to forge successful relationships with the media at critical incidents.

Introduction

Clashes between police and members of the media at critical incident scenes have become all too familiar and common—place law enforcement personnel scramble to deal with protecting evidence, aiding victims, and interviewing witnesses while onscene reporters and camera crews descend upon the situation to begin a piranha-like assault over local, state, or federal officers. The more blood and excitement these events produce, the more prominent the media blitz becomes. These repeated clashes are especially troubling in light of the many recent critical incidents experienced, from the traumatic September 11 attacks in New York City to the calculated sniper shootings in the Washington, DC area.

Critical incident scenes may include events such as natural disasters, hostage situations, suicides, high-profile homicides, hazardous materials spills and terrorist attacks. These scenes inherently have added significance for law enforcement officers and executives charged with responding to and maintaining control over these rare but often definitive crisis situations. Because of the unique nature of these high-profile emergency events, critical incident scenes provide an excellent context to explore the larger implications and effects of the relationship between the media and the police. Highly charged and emotionally gut-wrenching events can work to define and clarify a built-in conflict of interest that exists between the media and police officials—conflicts that have historically resulted in hostility, suspicion, and occasional violence.

This article uses interview data from one especially horrifying and salient critical incident, the 1995 bombing of the Murrah federal building in Oklahoma City, to provide a case study in police-media relations at critical incident scenes. We present the results of interviews conducted with various local police personnel and federal agents who were personally involved in securing the scene immediately following the bombing, as well as the subsequent trial of perpetrators Timothy McVeigh and Terry Nichols. In addition, one of the authors was present at both scenes and was responsible for providing police security. These interviews allow us to explore the process of communication that occurred between the media and police executives in Oklahoma City, and also provides a glimpse into the extent to which media pressures may affect police decision-making more generally. Finally, the interviews can supply useful information to law enforcement executives interested in finding ways to improve police-media relations.

Oklahoma City and the Historical Context of Police Media Relations

For many, the images that were seared into the American public's collective conscience in April 1995 remain indelible. The hulking, hollowed out frame of the Murrah federal building standing silent amid smoke and debris. Rescue personnel coming to the aid of injured, bloodied children. The horrified and stunned look of onlookers that mirrored the mood of a nation that day. The bombing was then the worst terrorist attack ever to occur on US soil, and the explosion of the massive fuel oil and fertiliser truck bomb that twisted steel and crushed concrete resulted not only in the death of 168 citizens, but also irrevocably altered the American public's sense of security.

If images of the horrific damage remain fresh, so too does the massive media presence that engulfed the site immediately following the event. As quickly as police and rescue personnel worked to secure the site, hordes of local and national journalists flocked excitedly to the scene, replete with bright lights, cameras, and an insatiable need for immediate coverage and information from authorities. The extensive media coverage would persist through search and rescue attempts, the investigation and ultimately the trial of the bombing suspects. The immediate and overwhelming presence of the media at the scene and the security problems that confronted police in Oklahoma City as a result of the bombing was not unique, but rather just another case in a decades-long struggle between law enforcement personnel and the media in the aftermath of critical incidents. Garner (1984) has characterised the historically stormy relationship as one comprising 'basic mistrust and perhaps even mutual dislike' between the two parties. Likewise, survey research has clearly identified significant and pronounced differences of opinion between members of the press and officers regarding the publication of crime news stories (Altschull, 1975; Selke & Bartoszek, 1984).

These points of conflict are not new, but rather appear to emanate from long-standing constitutional, occupational, and historical factors that have served to perpetuate struggles between police and members of the media over time. First, disagreements between the two groups are deeply embedded in the right to free speech outlined in the First Amendment to the US Constitution. In part, the First Amendment protects an individual's right to freedom of expression, including religious freedoms, rights to association, and freedoms of speech. The right to freedom of speech specifically prevents the government from interfering with the free expression of ideas; however, the US Supreme Court has limited these rights over time so that the right to freedom of expression is not absolute. For example, speech that has been deemed as libellous, obscene, or seditious is generally not protected under the First Amendment (Peltason, 1991). As a rule, the courts have attempted to balance the individual right to free speech with the government's (including the police) interest in promoting societal order and morality (Peltason).

While the rights associated with freedoms of expression generally extend to the actions of the press, it is important to note that the Constitution does not afford members of the media any special rights or privileges not granted to private individuals. For example, the First Amendment does not grant the media unabridged access to information or the right to interview members of the public (Peltason, 1991). Instead, courts have continually attempted to balance the right of the press to access information that it deems is in the 'public interest' with the rights of government to maintain order. For example, the Supreme Court has consistently upheld the media's right to access and report information relating to criminal trials, but has refrained from providing the media an absolute right to take pictures or publicly broadcast such proceedings (see *Richmond Newspapers, Inc.* v *Virginia;*[1] *Globe Newspaper Co.* v *Superior Court*[2]).

The issue of whether or not the media have a right to broadcast *publicly* specific information has undergone special scrutiny. In this regard, the court has ruled that 'there is no "unbridgeable" First Amendment right to broadcast comparable to the right of every individual to speak, write, or publish...' *(Red Lion Broadcasting Co.* v *Federal Communications Commission*[3]). Within this context, the court has tended to strike down laws designed to limit the broadcasting of information prior to its release. So too, the court has not been prone to permit the punishment of members of the media for publishing information that was found to be truthful and/or lawfully obtained *(Smith* v *Daily Mail Publishing* Co.[4]). Constitutional standards concerning the media's right to access information and individuals continue to evolve on a case-by- case basis and has recently become more complicated with the advent of new forms of media (eg cable television, the internet), so that the constitutional 'battle lines' between media and police concerning the right to broadcast specific information must be continually interpreted (Peltason, 1991).

In addition to the volatile legal context associated with the First Amendment, conflicts between the police and members of the media also appear to be influenced by deeply rooted occupational factors. First, there appear to be pre-existing distinctions in personality and orientation between law enforcement personnel and members of the media. For example, Selke and Bartoszek (1984) conducted a survey to explore the predisposition and general orientation of police cadets and journalism students regarding their prospective professions. Their results identified several attitudinal and perceptual differences in the way these two groups viewed the fields of law enforcement and journalism, suggesting that a large degree of suspicion and a lack of trust exists between members of these two professions even prior to their formal entry into these careers (Selke and Bartoszek).

These pre-existing differences seem to be reinforced as employees formally enter their respective fields, with the police academy serving to solidify negative media attitudes for rookie cops (Harris, 1973; Selke & Bartoszek, 1984) and journalism organisations doing likewise for cub reporters (Tuchman, 1978; Selke & Bartoszek). Altschull's (1975) survey of press representatives and law enforcement personnel specifically identified some of these differences. He found journalists to be more ideologically 'liberal' than police, and more likely to oppose police censorship and control over disputed areas of publication. Journalists were also found to believe in the value and credibility of 'unofficial' news tips more than police respondents did (Altschull).

The existing mutual distrust has also been fuelled by historical events that have worked to deepen the division between police and members of the media over time. In particular, the social and political turmoil of the 1960s seems to have served as a catalyst in the escalation of this 'undeclared war'. First, the media played a key role in identifying and investigating problems related to police corruption, abuses of power, and even criminal activity on the part of officers during this period (Sherman, 1974b). For example, the widely publicised story of New York City police officer Frank Serpico, initially broken by a *New York Times* reporter, stands as a continuing signpost to police misconduct during this period. Indeed, the media's role as the 'creator' of scandal designed as a tool to initiate disciplinary actions against wayward officers and changes in police organisations remains constant even today (Langworthy & Travis, 2003; Sherman 1974a).

Second, the social upheavals that arose during the civil rights movement, the Vietnam War, and the Watergate scandal thrust police into the difficult role of maintaining order in the face of riots. The news media, especially television, provided the public with views of police grappling with protesters in Chicago at the Democratic national convention, spraying fire hoses on demonstrators in Birmingham, Alabama, and attempting to quell riots in the aftermath of the shooting of Dr Martin Luther King. Clearly, the interaction between society's primary information system—the media—and society's primary system for enforcing behaviour—the police—had fostered a large degree of animosity by the end of the decade and created an atmosphere of mistrust between police and media personnel that remains today (Surrette, 1998).

More recently, the growth in competition that has occurred within the news media business in the last decade appears to have accelerated police-media conflicts (Surrette, 1998). Once consisting mostly of locally-operated, independent newspapers, the media industry has become increasingly dominated by vast global conglomerates that operate a wide array of different news outlets including not only print media, but also network television, cable television and internet media. The pace of media competition seems to have quickened with the advent of 24-hour cable news stations and their unending need to fill broadcast time with newsworthy features. With this growth in competition, news agencies find themselves in a struggle against one another for stories as well as customers. News outlets vie with one another to be the 'first on the story' in order to 'scoop' the competition and gain both additional viewers and advertising dollars (Surrette). In addition, a culture of paparazzi has developed where all means necessary to get a picture are used, often at the expense of personal privacy and dignity.

The media's insatiable appetite for news stands at odds with much of what police executives are challenged to accomplish in securing critical incident scenes. It is clearly within the individual officer's legitimate right to exercise his or her authority in order to provide for the safety of victims and bystanders in the aftermath of these critical incidents. Likewise, securing the area immediately surrounding a critical incident scene becomes vital to the apprehension of suspects and/or the restoration of order if the crisis situation remains ongoing (eg hostage situations, hazardous material spills). Finally, police authority must be employed in order to protect any remaining evidence that could aid in subsequent investigations.

It is within this volatile context that police officers from scores of federal, state, and local agencies confronted members of the local and national media on that fateful day in Oklahoma City. Both sides were there to accomplish important tasks, and the reporters and police officials who became an integral part of this event would provide an example of how the police and the media interact in critical incident scenes. What follows is a summary of excerpts derived from interviews conducted with individual law enforcement personnel present at the scene of the bombing, as well as information obtained in subsequent interviews of police assigned to the trials months later.

The Interviews

Data concerning law enforcement views regarding the media at the site of the Oklahoma City bombing and subsequent trials were obtained through interviews of supervisory or executive level police personnel directly involved in security duties at the sites. Five of the interview subjects were present at the bombing site, while six subjects were involved in policing the scene of the McVeigh and Nicholls trials. The interview subjects were employed by two separate federal agencies and one state agency. Interviews were conducted in person beginning in October 1998 and concluding in early 1999.

The interview subjects were chosen for several reasons. First, their collective positions both within the outer and intermediate perimeters of the security configuration at the sites involved significant interactions with both the national and local media outlets.[5] Second, the upper level positions of the subjects required them to formulate tactical decisions regarding the policing of the sites within the context of interacting with the media. Finally, these upper level officers were able to relate information communicated to them from their subordinates who were also involved in securing these scenes against media intrusions.

The interviews covered three main areas of information. The first portion of the interviews focused on the subjects' general orientations toward the media. This section attempted to uncover the subjects' preexisting beliefs regarding the relationship between the media and the police. The second portion of the interviews covered the specific content of the subjects' interactions with the media at the bombing site, and whether or not there was any conflict between the police and the media related to the security configuration and the media's access to news information at the site. The final part of the interviews focused on the subjects' reactions regarding these identical issues at the site of the trials of McVeigh and Nicholls.

Subjects' General Views of the Media

The subjects expressed both positive and negative general attitudes toward the media. The mixed reaction of the subjects suggests that the predominantly negative descriptions of police-media relations expressed in the prior literature still may exist, but that these attitudes may now be tempered with a degree of optimism that may be shaped by both a willingness on the part of law enforcement to confront this issue, as well as the recognition that conflict can be lessened by open and direct communications with the media. Additionally, the fact that the subjects were higher-ranking officials more acquainted with dealing with the media may have tempered their opinions.

Subjects who expressed generally negative attitudes toward the media clearly depicted the historical conflict. For example, one subject flatly stated that he 'did not like the media'. Another law enforcement official clearly restated the inherent occupational conflicts that exist between the two camps, suggesting that the media 'can hinder an investigation that is ongoing by releasing information that... could be used in subsequent interviews of suspects'. These generally negative viewpoints may also lead some law enforcement personnel to believe that the media often twist the facts surrounding events in order to portray the police in a negative light: 'The media attempt to sensationalize all of their stories if they can't get the news due to the police... then the media will make up facts and broadcast lies to the American public.'

While the negative perspectives expressed above could be viewed as prime examples of the historically conflicting nature of police-media relations, a majority of the subjects possessed more positive views. These subjects recognised the media's involvement in critical incident scenes as both necessary and integral parts of these events, and believed that police can use the presence of the media to their advantage when confronted with critical incident scenes: 'I think the mass media is a useful tool... and it is imperative that law enforcement has a working relationship with the media, which at times can be confusing.' For those who expressed positive orientations toward the media, this confusion can be lessened by two factors that can create successful relations in even the most difficult situations. First, these executives recognised the need for open and honest communications: 'You have to be up front with them... you have to be truthful.' Second, the responses emphasised that law enforcement personnel must communicate fair and thorough ground rules to the media in order to govern both the initial encounter and subsequent interactions: 'If at the very start you set certain rules and guidelines you agree to, you usually do not have a problem.'

Cooperation and Conflict at the Sites

The dual nature of these general views of the subjects toward the media—both positive and negative—may have worked to shape the nature of communication and the degree of cooperation that occurred at the actual bombing site. That is, the interviews revealed specific incidents of conflict between the police and the media; however, this conflict occurred within a general framework of cooperation between the two parties.

Again, the cooperation that occurred seemed to stem substantially from the communication of clear ground rules at the outset:

> Both you (the interviewer) and I are aware of certain situations up in Oklahoma City where people not necessarily in the mainstream press tried to go past what the rules were, tried to sneak through the security perimeters in an effort to get a scoop on the story. That was the exception, not the rule (at Oklahoma City). Your mainstream (media) will go by the rules… For the most part they have been very good. In a situation where you have an explosion, you set up your perimeters, you explain to them why they are there…

The clear consensus among the interviewees was that there was not much conflict at the site due to the fact that the media were told what the ground rules were from the start. Members of the media were also informed that they would be arrested if they chose to disregard these ground rules.

Another source of cooperation between the police and members of the media at the bomb site seemed to be the willingness of police executives to provide timely pieces of news to the media at regular intervals, effectively to 'give the media a bone' in order to avoid larger conflicts:

> Give them a little sound bite, that helps them out. If you give regular updates to them, that satisfies their needs. Of course you also, as bad as this may sound and knowing that they have deadlines, try to help them with those deadlines. (Then) they can meet their five and six and ten o'clock news reports… also give them sound bites for their broadcast. They are as happy as can be.

In this case, police executives appeared to recognise the needs of the media at critical incident scenes, including the need for at least a reasonable degree of newsworthy information that can be coupled with small amounts of video footage to satisfy viewers and sponsors alike (eg 'sound bites'). In this way, police executives at the bombing site were able to manage effectively the potential for conflict by mitigating the inherent friction that stems from the competing occupational roles that the media and police must play at critical incident scenes. The police are primarily at the scene to secure the site and investigate, but they also must recognise that the gravity related to critical incident scenes demands additional attention to the needs of the media.

Cooperation between the police and the media also appeared to be the rule at the site of the 1997 trials of McVeigh and Nicolls outside the federal courthouse in Denver, Colorado. This site appeared to contain the same potential for conflict between the mass media and the police because of the extensive coverage afforded to the trial and the extremely large contingent of reporters that followed the story from the bombing site to the courtroom months later. However, the potential for conflict at the trial site was obviously lessened by two factors. First, the trial site did not include the wreckage, immediate horror, and uncertainty that were indicative of the Oklahoma City site. Second, the police were aided in their quest for security by federal court orders regarding the lawful release of information.

If cooperation between the police and the media appeared to be the norm, it would be inaccurate to portray the relationship at Oklahoma City as one without conflict. Discussion with the subjects regarding these conflicts served two primary purposes. First, the points of contention between the police and the media that did occur during the Oklahoma City case accurately depict specific incidents where cooperation failed—where, for whatever reason, the police and members of the media neglected to address the potential sources of conflict described in the prior literature. Second, the instances of conflict cited by the interview subjects tended to involve highly prominent, national journalists. The individuals that helped to develop these conflicts could, by their notoriety, function as highly visible examples of the potential problems police administrators must plan for in critical incident scenes.

One subject described his personal involvement in 'detaining' Geraldo Rivera, the long-time critically acclaimed but highly controversial journalist whose career has included stints with ABC News, the prime time investigative show '20/20', as well as his own talk show. At the time, Rivera was covering the bombing for Fox News. The interview subject began by providing an overview of his experiences with the media at the bombing site:

> We had a problem keeping the news media out of the bomb site. We had conflicts with stories... several disagreements with stories that they produced during the investigation... They were always, always around the bomb site trying to get in, working, trying to get information as to what was going on.

This combative scenario finally culminated in the detainment of Rivera and his subsequent transport to the city jail. Rivera had attempted to infiltrate the security perimeter dressed in a white physician's coat and carrying a stethoscope. Medical personnel at the site were constantly interacting with investigators in order to render aid to victims and determine the cause of death for those who were deceased. The interview subject recognised Rivera despite the disguise, drew his side arm, and handcuffed Rivera. He was turned over to United States marshals. Rivera was later released without charge in order to ease tensions between the police and the media.

Another specific incident of conflict arose at the site of the subsequent trials. On the date of the initial hearing, police and the Tenth Circuit Court of Appeals established a rule that no media filming was to occur immediately in front of the court building for security reasons. Ted Koppel, an ABC news veteran of 24 years' standing and longtime anchor of the award-winning late-night news programme *Nightline*, and his producers attempted to circumvent this rule by conducting an interview with Oklahoma City teens and their reaction to the bombing. Federal police approached Koppel and advised him of the rule. The media contingent became visibly irate and combative towards the law enforcement personnel; however, calm was restored when the interview was terminated after Koppel and his crew were warned of the possibility of arrest for violations of security measures.

Media and police personnel also experienced less notorious instances of conflict at the sites. The subjects related that negative reporting on the part of the media towards the police was, at times, a point of contention. One specific report that criticised the 'lacklustre' response of fire and rescue personnel was specifically cited. Some subjects also believed that there was a lack of news regarding positive law enforcement actions at the scene, including a detailing of how police there tended to and consoled victims. Several of the subjects related heartfelt experiences with some of the victims. These stories were not always broadcast on the six o'clock news, but they are commonplace at critical incident scenes like Oklahoma City:

> This woman was absolutely devastated. You could tell by the way she was acting, the tears, the emotion, the circumstances surrounding her brother's death. I allowed her into the compound… She said a few prayers, cried on my shoulder, talked out loud to her brother. We sat there for a half-hour to forty-five minutes in complete silence… What I did made an impact on her. It helped her deal with the loss. Was I supposed to [let her in]? Did I violate some rule about people being in the compound? Yes, but it was what I could do to help people with their loss.

Mitigating conflict: lessons from Oklahoma City

Critical incident scenes like the Oklahoma City bombing site are unique in terms of their emotionality. Hostage situations, natural disasters, high-profile homicides, and terrorist actions result in emergency situations that are filled with danger, hostility, and grief beyond those found in normal law enforcement circumstances. The police are confronted with the challenges of aiding victims, controlling bystanders, and providing security for investigation and resolution. These challenges are often faced in the presence of a large media contingent whose fundamental goal (ie get the story at all costs) is at odds with that of the police. Administrators must control the potential for conflict with the media in order to secure these situations and avoid undue negative publicity. While critical incident scenes are certainly not the norm, the September 11th attacks and the continuing war on terror suggest that they may become more commonplace in the immediate future. As the potential for an increase in the number of critical incident scenes grows, knowledge concerning these incidents and strategies to deal with them effectively become increasingly essential to police administrators. In the interest of accomplishing these goals, as well as clearly defining what these cases entail, Duda (1999) provides a comprehensive discussion of the common factors

Table 3.1. Factors to consider at critical incident scenes

√	Massive confusion
	Including traffic disruptions, school and business closings, and widespread public confusion.
√	Soaring Public Interest
	As a direct result of intense media scrutiny. This factor necessarily raises the stakes concerning police decision-making.
√	Situational exigencies
	Including provisions for victims in need of immediate medical aid, the need to secure the scene and search for evidence and possible suspects, and the mitigation of ongoing potential danger.
√	Information Management
	Including interpretation and dissemination of rapid and often conflicting press reports concerning suspects, victims, witnesses, as well as unconfirmed information leaks from other sources such as emergency personnel.
√	Regulation of External Influences
	Such as reporters, commentators, political figures, and regulators, many of whom may know very little about the actual operation at hand. These influences have the potential to influence wider public perceptions concerning the critical incident, and in turn police credibility at the scene.

Note. Information in Table 3.1 adapted from Jane's Crisis Communications Handbook (2002).

that administrators must consider in order to manage critical incident scenes effectively. Table 3.1 provides a summary of the most salient factors adapted from Duda (1999):

In addition to recognising the common problems associated with most of these events, the Oklahoma City interview data may also be used to suggest more specific strategies to mitigate the potential for media conflict. First, the interview subjects consistently pointed to the need for police executives to formulate and communicate to the media clear 'rules of engagement'. That is, police need to set boundaries in terms of where the media will be located at the scene, as well as when and how the media will be provided information. This 'rule of engagement' also implies that the police will be forthcoming in providing a certain degree of information that is delivered in a timely manner so that the media can fulfil their objectives at critical incident scenes. Second, the mitigation of potential conflict involves forthright actions on the part of both the police and the media. The only instances of true conflict at the bombing and trial sites were created when these 'rules of engagement' were broken. If they are adhered to, these ground rules work to mitigate conflict by addressing the opposing occupational needs of both police and the media.

The clear definition and communication of 'rules of engagement' between law enforcement and media personnel may be aided by the utilisation of a public information officer (PIO). The primary mission of the PIO is to act as a conduit between the police and media.

As the police liaison to the media, the PIO should be well versed in writing, public speaking, and the legal aspects associated with the rights of the media. In many medium-sized and small police departments, the police chief or the highest-ranking officer may be the most appropriate choice to perform these duties (Garner, 1984). The PIO is responsible for the timely dispersal of police department information to the press. The position should also entail addressing any complaints the media may have regarding police practices. In connection with this, the PIO can also relay information concerning the 'proper' conduct of media members. In critical incident situations, the PIO is responsible for bringing order to chaos—for ensuring that police-media relations do not result in conflict. Table 3.2 is a list of the primary duties of the PIO in critical incident scenes adapted from Garner:

The issue of police-media relations has recently gained increased research attention, and a growing list of resources is now available to police administrators that would aid communication and cooperation at critical incident scenes as well as less notorious events. For example, *Jane's Crisis Communications Handbook* (2002), a resource that provides comprehensive and practical procedures aimed at assisting both corporate and public sector media relations, could be used as a general guidebook for those hoping to create order in the aftermath of emergencies. Similar to the views expressed by the Oklahoma City subjects, the *Handbook* emphasises the need for some type of 'principal spokesperson' to engage media personnel at the scene.

This spokesperson should strive to follow a range of common sense guidelines including: (1) notifying families first of any injuries and shielding those individuals from immediate media pressures; (2) ensuring that law enforcement is the first and primary source of information concerning the incident, rather than independent 'experts' or competing media organisations; (3) reserving press conferences for only the most important announcements; (4) refraining from discussing undetermined or unverified issues; and (5) avoiding using messages that could encourage 'copy cat' acts.

Information from those who worked in the aftermath of the Oklahoma City bombing, as well as a host of additional sources, suggests that conflict is not an inevitable byproduct of the occupational differences between the police and the media, but rather, critical incident scenes

Table 3.2. Duties of the Public Information Officer (PIO)

√	Communicate the established perimeter to the media
√	Establish a media briefing area ('bullpen') that will serve as a specified location for news briefings. The distance of the 'bullpen' area from the incident scene needs to be distant enough to ensure media safety, but proximate enough to facilitate photographic access to the scene.
√	Transmit formal written copies of existing law enforcement standard operating procedures for critical incidents in general, as well as evolving procedures for the particular incident in question
√	Establish time frames for the dissemination of information to the media and maintenance of that schedule.

Note. Information in Table 3.2 adapted from Garner (1984).

can be managed so that police officers and reporters alike can cooperate given the appropriate framework. This framework is provided through clear ground rules and open communication, and may be aided by the establishment of PIOs who can create and maintain these avenues of communication. These recommendations stress the notion that the media are essentially a bridge between the police and the *public,* with the public encompassing the true audience of concern for law enforcement administrators. This suggests that improved police- media relations would not only create more order and security in times of crisis or critical incidents, but also better communication and understanding between police and the citizens whom they serve.

Notes

1. *Richmond Newspapers Inc.* v *Virginia* 448 U.S. 555 (1980).

2. *Globe Newspaper Co.* v *Superior Court,* 457 U.S. 596 (1982).

3. *Red Lion Broadcasting Co.* v *Federal Communications Commission,* 395 U.S. 367 (1969).

4. *Smith* v *Daily Mail Publishing Co.,* 443 U.S. 97 (1979).

5. According to the interview subjects, the security configuration at the bombing site consisted of concentric layers of security made up of an outer, intermediate, and inner perimeter. The outer perimeter primarily consisted of officers from various Oklahoma state agencies. The intermediate perimeter consisted of federal officers and special agents from the Federal Protective Service. The inner perimeter was policed by US marshals.

References

Altschull, J. (1975). The Press and the Police: News Flow and Ideology. *Journal of Police Science and Administration 3,* 733–747.

Garner, G. (1984). *The Police Meet the Press* (1st ed.). Springfield, IL: Thomas.

Harris, R. (1973). *The Police Academy.* New York: Wiley and Sons.

Jane's Crisis Communications Handbook (2002). December.

Langworthy, H., & Travis, L. F., III (2003). *Policing in America: A Balance of Forces,* (3rd ed.). Upper Saddle River, NJ: Prentice Hall.

Peltason, J.W. (1991). *Understanding the Constitution* (12th ed.). New York: Harcourt Brace Jovanovich.

Selke,W, & Bartoszek, G. (1984). Police and Media Relations: The Seeds of Conflict. *Criminal Justice Review 2,* 25–30

Sherman, L.W (1974a). *Police Corruption: A Sociological Perspective.* Garden City, NY: Anchor Books.

Sherman, L.W. (1974b). The Sociology and Social Reform of the American Police. *Journal of Police Science and Administration, 2,* 255–262.

Surrette, R. (1998). *Media, Crime, and Criminal Justice: Images and Realities* (2nd ed.). Belmont, CA: Wadsworth.

Tuchman, G. (1978). *Making News: A Study in the Construction of Reality.* New York: Free Press.

SECTION TWO

Critical Incident Stress Management

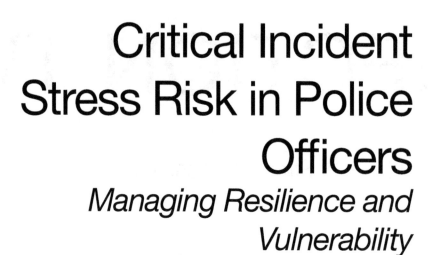

Critical Incident Stress Risk in Police Officers
Managing Resilience and Vulnerability

DOUGLAS PATON

G rowing empirical and theoretical evidence for positive and adaptive outcomes signals a need for an alternative conceptualization of the critical incident stress process in police officers. Using a risk management framework, this article conceptualizes critical incident stress in a way that accommodates both positive (e.g., posttraumatic growth) and negative outcomes (e.g., learned avoidance of threat situations). It identifies resilience and vulnerability factors (at personal, team, and environmental levels) and discusses how they interact with incident demands to affect stress risk during

Douglas Paton, "Critical Incident Stress Risk in Police Officers: Managing Resilience and Vulnerability," *Traumatology*, vol. 12, no. 3, pp. 198-206. Copyright © 2006 by American Psychological Association. Reprinted with permission.

the response and reintegration ph ases of incident response. Strategies to influence resilience and vulnerability factors are discussed.

Keywords: critical incident stress; risk management; resilience; vulnerability; learning

Police officers are regularly exposed to critical incidents (emergencies and disasters).
Although this work is traditionally viewed as a precursor to the development of acute and
chronic posttraumatic stress reactions, growing evidence for its association with positive
outcomes calls for a reappraisal of this aspect of police work (Moran, 1999; Moran &
Colless, 1995; Paton, Violanti, & Smith, 2003). Positive outcomes include exercising
professional skills to achieve highly meaningful outcomes, posttraumatic growth, enhanced
professional capability, a greater appreciation for family, and an enhanced sense of control
over significant adverse events. Furthermore, a growing body of evidence suggests that
growth and deficit outcomes are discrete and coexist (Hart & Wearing, 1995; Huddleston,
Paton, & Stephens, 2006 [this issue]; Linley & Jospeh, 2004; Tedeschi & Calhoun, 2003;
Tugade & Frederickson, 2004). If a comprehensive account of this aspect of police work is
to be forthcoming, a new conceptualization of critical incident stress, and one capable of
accommodating these diverse outcomes, is required.

This article proposes that the risk management paradigm provides such a framework.
The article commences with an introduction to risk management and the qualities that
render it appropriate as a vehicle for a comprehensive conceptualization of traumatic stress
reactivity. Then the article identifies the potential content of a model and how it could be
used to manage traumatic stress in police officers.

Developing a Stress Risk Management Model

The starting point for this process is recognition that traumatic stress symptoms (e.g.,
intrusive ideation) reflect the experience of a state of psychological disequilibrium as a
result of a person's inability to organize elements of their atypical experience in meaningful
ways (Janoff-Bulman, 1992; Paton, 1994). The event that triggers the disequilibrium acts
as a catalyst for change. According to the evidence introduced above, the new equilibrium
state that emerges following a traumatic experience could be characterized by growth (e.g.,
posttraumatic growth) or loss (e.g., learned avoidance of threat situations). Which outcome
occurs is less a function of the experience per se and more a result of how it interacts with
elements that increase an officer's susceptibility to experiencing loss from exposure to a
critical incident (i.e., increase vulnerability) and those that facilitate adaptation and growth
(Paton et al., 2003; Violanti & Paton, 2006).

If the factors that influence stress risk can be identified, police organizations will be
in a better position to make choices about the outcomes their officers can experience. To
guide organizational analysis and action, a framework capable of integrating these issues is
required. The risk concept is an appropriate candidate for this role.

Although its contemporary usage tends to focus on loss, the term *risk* also encompasses
notions of anticipation and resilience. This confers on the risk management paradigm a
capacity to encapsulate both growth/adaptation and deficit/loss outcomes (Dake, 1992;

Hood & Jones, 1996) in models of traumatic stress processes. Within risk management models, risk is represented as an interaction between hazards and resilience resources and vulnerability factors. If these factors can be identified and quantified, a framework capable of accommodating multiple outcomes and estimating the probabilities of positive and negative outcomes will be available.

First, sources of hazard must be recognized and understood. Hazard analysis involves identifying the event (e.g., body recovery) and operational (e.g, decision making under conditions under uncertainty) demands that officers encounter. Second, risk assessment examines how hazards interact with resilience and vulnerability factors to estimate the outcome of exposure to a given event (i.e., to estimate risk under specific circumstances). The acceptability or otherwise of the ensuing estimate of risk informs the development of risk management policies and practices required for effective traumatic stress risk reduction in police organizations. That is, if hazard, resilience, and vulnerability factors are known, choices can be made within the risk management process through better planning and preparedness to reduce the prevalence of vulnerability factors and increase those that enhance resilience. It is to a discussion of candidates for these factors that this article now turns. In doing so, the objective is not to produce a comprehensive inventory. Rather, the goal is to select examples to illustrate how the model could be applied.

Applying Stress Risk Management to Police Organizations

CRITICAL INCIDENT HAZARDS

Critical incidents expose personnel to several factors that can become psychological hazards because of their potential to threaten officers' psychological integrity (Paton, 1997). For example, because they threaten perceived control, events whose cause is attributed to acts of omission (e.g., building collapse from poor workmanship) or commission (e.g., terrorist bombing) are more significant hazards than their natural counterparts (MacLeod & Paton, 1999). Uncertainty regarding threat duration, length of involvement, or recurrence (e.g., being secondary targets of terrorist attacks) are hazards. So too is personal danger (e.g., working in unsafe buildings, exposure to toxic chemicals, biological or radiation hazards) and having to operate under high time pressures.

These hazards are critical in the sense that they force officers and organizations to confront assumptions derived from previous experiences and operations. It is the atypical nature of these events that underpins their potential to create psychological disequilibrium (Janoff-Bulman, 1992; Paton, 1994; Tugade & Frederickson, 2004). According to the risk management model proposed here, whether the new equilibrium state that ensues following the experience is characterized by growth or loss is a function of how the hazard experience interacts with vulnerability and resilience factors.

When officers respond to events, they bring their personal characteristics to bear on the problems encountered. They must also be able to exercise their duties under nonroutine circumstances, and they respond as members of a police organization. Consequently, factors that influence stress risk will emanate from personal, operational, and organizational sources. Discussion of candidates for these factors commences with those at the individual level.

INDIVIDUAL RESILIENCE AND VULNERABILITY

Scotti, Beach, Northrop, Rode, and Forsyth (1995) described individual vulnerability as emanating from three sources: biological (e.g., genetic, altered physiological reactivity from prior traumatic exposure), historical (e.g., preexisting psychopathology), and psychological (e.g., social skills and problem-solving deficits). In regard to dispositional resilience, evidence exists to demonstrate how factors such as hardiness, emotional stability, self-awareness, tolerance for ambiguity, and self-efficacy can enhance resilience (Flin, 1996; Linley & Joseph, 2004; MacLeod & Paton, 1999; Paton et al., 2003). Knowledge of these factors can be used to, for example, select officers for special high-risk projects (e.g., terrorist task force) and prioritize officers for postevent intervention. In addition to these dispositional factors, traumatic stress risk is also influenced by individual differences in how officers make sense of their experience.

Officers bring to any specific incident ways of interpreting experiences that reflect their history, training, and the culture of the organization of which they are members. A combination of these diverse influences means that individual differences between officers with regard to how they interpret events will influence stress risk. For example, the scale of a critical incident (particularly terrorist events) can limit opportunities for effective action (e.g., as was the case at the World Trade Center and at Shankesville following the 9/11 attacks). Vulnerability increases if an inability to act as expected (e.g., because of the scale of the loss) is interpreted as personal inadequacy rather than attributing it to environmental constraints beyond an individual's control. This process has been labeled *performance guilt* (Raphael, 1986). However, training that develops realistic outcome expectations, assists positive interpretation (e.g., body recovery assists families to begin the grieving process, not a rescue failure), promotes an ability to differentiate personal and situational constraints, and provides interpretive processes that review experiences as learning opportunities that enhance future competence increases resilience (Alexander & Wells, 1991; Dunning, 2003; Paton, 1994; Paton & Jackson, 2002; Thompson, 1993).

Simulation exercises can assist officers to develop mental models that facilitate their capacity to impose coherence on atypical and complex emergencies. Simulations provide opportunities to understand and review response activities and develop realistic performance expectations. They also help increase knowledge of stress reactions and provide opportunities for officers to rehearse strategies to deal with them (Crego & Spinks, 1997; Paton, 1994; Paton & Jackson, 2002; Tugade & Frederickson, 2004).

Developing these more sophisticated psychological structures requires two inputs. One concerns the systematic analysis of the physical and psychological demands and challenges that officers could encounter when confronting critical incidents. The second involves designing simulations capable of reconciling these event demands (e.g., scale of damage, rapid role change) with the competencies (e.g., hazard identification and interpretation, adapting plans accordingly, team and multiagency operation, information and decision management) required to increase the likelihood of officer adaptation (Paton, 1994; Paton et al., 1999, 2003).

When confronting critical incidents, officers not only have to make sense of their experiences but they have to be able to operate effectively under these circumstances. That is, some measure of operational resilience, the capacity to conduct appointed tasks under atypical circumstances, is also required. This issue is illustrated here with reference to making decisions under crisis conditions and working in multiagency teams.

OPERATIONAL RESILIENCE

Information and decision management. During critical incidents, officers can be called on to act in complex environments characterized by uncertainty and limited and often ambiguous information. For trained personnel, however, crises can enhance alertness and thinking skills (Flin, 1996). The question then becomes one of identifying the competencies officers require if they are to realize the benefits of this circumstance. An important adaptive competence in this context is situational awareness—a capability to operate in complex contexts by extracting just those cues necessary to identify appropriate courses of action (Endsley & Garland, 2000). Although situational awareness allows officers to prioritize issues for action, putting them into practice requires competence in crisis decision making.

Naturalistic decision making, in which an officer recognizes the type of situation encountered and, from previous experience, selects an appropriate course of action, is highly adaptive in events characterized by substantial time pressure and high risk (Flin, Salas, Strub, & Martin, 1997). Because situational awareness and success in naturalistic decision making is a function of the ability to match current and prior situations, decision effectiveness is enhanced with more options to match. This ability can be developed through experience or simulation (Flin et al., 1997).

In complex emergencies, officers rarely work alone. Rather, they will function as part of a team. One outcome from analyses of 9/11 events and subsequent simulations (e.g., TOPOFF 1-3) was recognition that, although representing an important response resource, working within interagency teams can also influence stress risk.

TEAM AND INTERAGENCY OPERATIONS

Simply bringing together representatives of agencies who have had little contact with one another under normal circumstances (as was the case in 9/11) can increase stress vulnerability (Department of Homeland Security, 2003; Federal Emergency Management Agency, 2004; Flin & Arbuthnot, 2002; Grant, Hoover, Scarisbrick-Hauser, & Muffet, 2003; Jackson, Baker, Ridgely, Bartis, & Linn, 2003; Kendra & Wachtendorf, 2003; Paton et al., 2003). These authors discussed how operating in ad hoc teams can increase interagency conflict, result in a blurring of roles and responsibilities, and fuel frustration and feelings of inadequacy and helplessness.

Effective interagency teams can be developed using liaison mechanisms and integrating their respective roles through interagency planning and team development (Flin & Arbuthnott, 2002). Consequently, risk management planning should extend beyond the organization to accommodate the interorganizational relationships that could emerge in multiagency emergency response situations (e.g., terrorist events; Department of Homeland Security, 2003). In particular, planning and exercising together can reduce a tendency toward turf protection (e.g., to safeguard an organization's resource base) and increase agency willingness to work collaboratively (Paton et al., 1999).

Extensive joint planning and teamwork activity involving team members can enhance stress resilience (Brannick, Salas, & Prince, 1997; Flin, 1996; Paton et al., 1999, 2003), with good information sharing being a prominent element of this strategy. In effective teams, members provide more unprompted information, increasing a capability for proactive response management through better decision making and resource allocation (Entin & Serfaty, 1999). For this to occur effectively, team members must share a team mental model that facilitates the provision of goal-related information required by decision makers at critical periods (Cooke, Salas, Cannon-Bowers, & Stout, 2000).

As the level of teamwork and planning activity increases, personnel develop progressively similar mental models of response environments and the roles and tasks performed within them. This, in turn, increases implicit information sharing during high workload periods, enhancing team capacity to respond to complex and emergent demands encountered when responding to critical incidents (Paton & Jackson, 2002; Stout, Cannon-Bowers, Salas, & Milanovich, 1999).

The overall objective of this process is to increase participants' understanding of their respective contributions to the same plan and increase their shared understanding of each member's role in the response. This contributes to their capacity to share a common understanding of evolving events, work toward common goals over time, and, importantly, to anticipate the needs of those with whom they are collaborating (Flin, 1996). The latter is crucial to effective decision making in multiagency teams.

The concept of distributed decision making recognizes the need for contributions from people who differ with respect to their profession, functions, roles, and expertise; that they may be in different locations; or that they may be involved in different levels (e.g., operational vs. tactical) of decision making (Paton & Flin, 1999). Planning and training simulations designed to support this capacity should be based on a comprehensive hazard analysis (to provide realistic, challenging scenarios), involve key agencies, and be followed by critical evaluation.

The evaluation process should also consider how the relationship between officers and the police organization influences well-being. It is important to remember that officers respond to events as members of police organizations whose culture and the procedures and practices that flow from it influence their thoughts and actions, including how they experience critical incidents (Johnston & Paton, 2003; Weick, 1995). The organizational context can thus represent a significant and often neglected influence on traumatic stress risk (Huddleston et al., 2006; Paton & Violanti, 2006).

The management context. Officers' stress risk is affected by organizational culture and the procedures and practices that it promotes. For example, police agencies that persist in using established operational and decision procedures (even when responding to different and urgent crisis demands) and place protecting the organization from criticism or blame above safeguarding the well-being of its officers increases stress vulnerability (Gist & Woodall, 2000). Similarly, procedures such as a lack of consultation, poor communication, and excessive paperwork increase stress vulnerability (Hart & Wearing, 1995; Huddleston et al., 2006).

In contrast, police organizations that develop response systems and procedures that devolve responsibility to officers and that support flexible, consultative leadership practices that ensure that role and task assignments reflect incident demands enhance resilience (Alexander & Wells, 1991; Gist & Woodall, 2000; Paton, 1994). Similarly, organizations that emphasize recognition of good work and delegate responsibility increase the likelihood of officers' experiencing salutary outcomes (Hart & Wearing, 1995; Huddleston et al., 2006). Another important finding to emerge from this work has been recognition that the positive and negative aspects of climate coexist, exercise an influence on different posttrauma outcomes simultaneously, and must be managed accordingly. Recognition of the significant role of organizational culture is important in other respects. In particular, it defines the context within which officers review their critical incident experiences and deal with their reactions. The term *reintegration* is used to describe this period.

Stress Risk During Reintegration

During reintegration, as officers return to routine duties, stress risk management involves managing the emotional correlates of an event and rendering it meaningful. In regard to the former, support practices that assist positive resolution and growth are discussed elsewhere (Dunning, 2003; Tedeschi & Calhoun, 2003). Although the management of adverse experience (e.g., debriefing) has dominated postevent practice, several studies have demonstrated that this exercises a lesser influence on recovery than organizational culture and family dynamics (Huddleston et al., 2006; Paton & Violanti, 2006).

Attention to family issues is important both for their sake and in regard to their role as a recovery resource. In addition to its emanating from dealing with their experience of a partners' involvement in a critical incident, organizational issues (e.g., shift work) are prominent family risk factors (Shakespeare-Finch, Paton, & Violanti, 2003). Practices that reduce family risk and enhance their capacity as a support resource (e.g., family-friendly policies and support groups, including family members in recovery planning) should be included in risk management programs.

The period of transition from crisis to routine work and family life poses a unique set of demands on officers. Vulnerability is not restricted to those who have had negative event experiences. For example, officers may experience feelings of loss as they leave a period of rewarding personal or professional performance. Readjusting to routine work, dealing with event-related issues and reporting pressures, catching up with any backlog, and dealing with any legal and sociolegal aspects of the response may also affect postevent stress risk. The implications for reintegration, however, are a function of how they interact with support resources and organizational practices and culture.

INTERPERSONAL SUPPORT AND COHESION

Although generally considered to ameliorate stress reactions, this need not always be the case (Paton & Stephens, 1996; Solomon & Smith, 1994). Solomon and Smith (1994) discussed how the demands on a social network for support occur at a time when all members may have support needs. This makes support provision a highly stressful event in itself, potentially reducing both its availability and quality. This problem can be managed by providing social support via coworker and peer support groups (Paton, 1997; Williams, 1993). This resource should be developed to ensure its members can manage all the issues (e.g., accommodating others' perspectives, rumination, counterfactual thinking) that characterize the reintegration experience (Gist & Woodall, 2000; MacLeod & Paton, 1999; Paton & Stephens, 1996).

Cohesive teams can constitute a natural resilience resource (Higgins, 1994; Park, 1998). However, cohesion can contribute to vulnerability if situational constraints (e.g., people dying because equipment or response time was inadequate) result in a response being perceived as less effective than anticipated. Under these conditions, officers may find it difficult to perceive the positive characteristics in the group necessary to maintain a positive social identity. If this occurs, support networks break down, a negative social identity develops, and stress vulnerability increases (Paton & Stephens, 1996; Solomon & Smith, 1994). To counter this, team processes that facilitate the realistic interpretation of circumstances, actively differentiate personal and situational response factors, and encourage interpretation of experience as an opportunity for personal and professional growth are required (Gist & Woodall, 2000; Lyons, Mickelson, Sullivan, & Coyne, 1998; Park, 1998; Paton & Stephens, 1996).

Lyons et al. (1998) used the term *communal coping* to describe how teams can create a stronger, more resilient response than can be achieved by individuals. They argued that communal coping requires officers' shared acceptance of event-related problems (e.g., taking collective responsibility for response issues) and discussion on cooperative action to resolve problems. The latter can occur in formal review sessions and in informal day-to-day interactions between team members as they return to work. Acknowledging and building on effective collaboration during the crisis, and working together after the crisis, to develop understanding and better preparedness for future crises will facilitate communal coping, resilience, and future integrated performance. Stress risk is also influenced by the organizational culture within which reintegration occurs.

Vulnerability increases if experience is interpreted in an organizational culture that discourages emotional disclosure, focuses on attributing blame to staff, or minimizes the significance of peoples' reactions or feelings (Paton & Stephens, 1996; MacLeod & Paton, 1999). The likelihood of positive reintegration is heightened if managers work with staff to reconcile the personal impact of the event with the process of returning to work.

Senior officers can assist adaptation by helping officers appreciate that they performed to the best of their ability and reducing performance guilt by realistically reviewing how situational factors constrained performance (Alexander & Wells, 1991; MacLeod & Paton, 1999; Paton, 1997). Senior officers can also facilitate positive resolution by assisting staff to identify the strengths that helped them deal with the incident and building on this to plan how future events can be dealt with more effectively. Thus, risk management programs should review the climate of relationships between managers and staff and determine its implications for response and reintegration (Gist & Woodall, 2000). Such analyses can inform risk assessment by, for example, identifying response constraints within organizational systems and procedures (e.g., lack of policy and procedures for managing critical incident stress, inadequate reintegration management). This activity can promote future response effectiveness and contribute to a resilient organizational climate. This observation highlights the need for police organizations to review their direct contribution to traumatic stress risk.

Police Organizations and Mitigating Traumatic Stress Risk

As is the case for their officers, a crisis can be a catalyst for change for police organizations. A capability for effective response, however, need not always exist. Organizations can respond in one of several ways.

At one end of the spectrum lies the nonresponse. This occurs when bureaucratic inertia, vested political interests, and centralized power and authority conspire to block change and, indeed, sow the seeds of future and more complex crises (Gunderson et al., 1995). Under these circumstances, organizations assume that crises happen only to other organizations, that the organization is too big and powerful to be affected by a disaster, or that the impact will be sufficiently small, allowing prompt recovery (Mitroff & Anagnos, 2001). Ignoring signals of potential or actual problems and therefore failing to plan for crises increases vulnerability. However, the emergence of complex terrorist events on the critical incident landscape has increased a need for organizations to recognize that they face an operating environment whose characteristics can differ radically from that which has historically prevailed. Simply acknowledging the existence of this may not, however, be enough.

A second category (Gunderson, Holling, & Light, 1995) is one in which a police organization accepts a need for change but lacks the experience to do so effectively. This can occur as a consequence of failing to consider risk from nonroutine events because managerial expectations regarding operating conditions and outcomes have become entrenched and insulated from environmental input (Berkes, Colding, & Folke, 2003; Paton & Wilson, 2001). By attempting to render complex, novel events understandable by making them fit in with previous experience (e.g., assuming that existing procedures are sufficient to manage complex terror events), police organizations may overlook threats or initiate inadequate actions, reducing their ability to match their capabilities to changing environmental demands (Grant et al., 2003; Jackson et al., 2003; Kendra & Wachtendorf, 2003). The rise of terrorism, in particular, makes the development of new ways of thinking about police work, the relationship between police organizations and the environment, and the relationship between the organization and its officers very important.

If organizations do not start to "think outside the square," it will be difficult for senior officers to consider, far less develop, the means to confront crises that arise from these new and more complex environmental realities. Similar problems can arise if police organizations fail to learn the lessons from previous events. The consequent implementation of untried actions, even while recognizing a need for change, can enhance resilience or it can increase vulnerability and exacerbate the loss of adaptive capacity (Berkes et al., 2003). That is, the outcome, greater resilience or heightened vulnerability, is determined more by chance than by sound planning and good judgment.

Berkes et al. (2003) emphasized that the development of adaptive organizational capacity requires learning from the experience of failure and recognition that new environmental realities require new ways of thinking. Not only must the organization learn to live with risk, it must develop strategies to learn from any crises and failures that occur. It involves

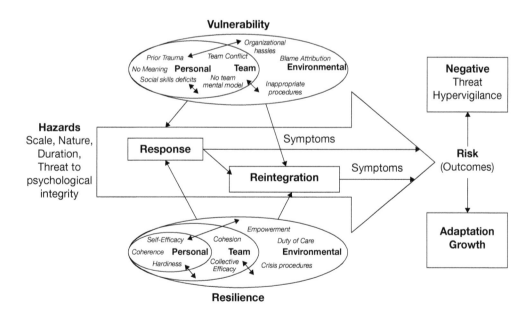

Figure 1. Stress risk management framework. The relative balance of resilience and vulnerability factors mobilized to confront the challenges posed by hazards predict the balance of growth and negative outcomes.

accepting that failing to plan for failure creates risks comparable to failing to plan to succeed. Recognition of the importance of institutional learning leads to a third strategy, one capable of contributing to resilience.

According to Berkes et al. (2003), this involves several activities. First, the memory of prior crises and the lessons learned must be incorporated into institutional memory. Second, it requires the rehearsal of lessons learned within a paradigm shift based on the recognition that nonroutine events require innovative operating practices (e.g., devolved responsibility, specialized reporting procedures) and that some events might overwhelm organizational capacity. Recognition of the latter makes it easier to appreciate the need for dedicated critical incident training and decision making (see above) within the stress risk management process. Finally, these activities lead to the development of new rules and procedures. The effectiveness of this institutional learning approach can be enhanced using simulations to facilitate the learning process, challenge complacency, enhance adaptive capacity, and encourage creative decision making (Berkes et al., 2003; Kendra & Wachtendorf, 2003; Paton & Jackson, 2002; Paton & Wilson, 2001).

Conclusion

The risk management paradigm affords an opportunity for officers and police organizations to make choices about traumatic stress outcomes associated with the experience of critical incidents. Although described here sequentially, the application of the risk management model will involve action at all levels to ensure that risk management is as inclusive as possible (Figure 1). Figure 1 describes the elements of the stress risk management model. The above discussion encompasses only a sample of factors that influence risk, and additional work is required to develop a comprehensive inventory.

The model provides a basis for auditing existing cultures, practices, and competencies. Of course, the degree to which it is applied will be qualified by several organizational characteristics. Some organizations will have some of these measures in place, some will have to develop them, and others may not be in a position to do so. For the first two groups, the risk management model can be used to inform their risk management agenda. For those in the last group, the model can be used to inform their assessment of residual risk (Violanti & Paton, 2006). This process identifies issues that are significant predictors of risk but that cannot be managed within the risk management process.

Knowledge of residual risk can guide several risk management initiatives for police organizations that are not in a position to act on the model. For example, it can be used to guide the development of collaborative training and simulation exercises with other organizations in a similar position to themselves. It can also furnish information that can be used to, for example, advise officers of sources of risk so they are better informed of the causes of their own reactions or advise of issues that may need to be taken into account within counseling sessions. Or it can inform strategic planning through, for example, providing an evidence-based platform for lobbying for additional resources.

Because critical incidents represent catalysts for change, traumatic stress risk management should be viewed as an iterative process that encompasses personal and organizational learning through the application of selection, training, and cultural and operational practices that promote and sustain resilience and growth. When this happens, estimates of staff capability to deal with job demands will increase substantially, as will confidence in the planning and policies that define organizational responsibility and action.

References

Alexander, D. A., & Wells, A. (1991). Reactions of police officers to body handling after a major disaster: A before and after comparison. *British Journal of Psychiatry, 159,* 517–555.

Berkes, F., Colding, J., & Folke, C. (2003). *Navigating socialecological systems: Building resilience for complexity and change.* Cambridge, UK: Cambridge University Press.

Brannick, M., Salas, E., & Prince, C. (Eds.). (1997). *Team performance, assessment and measurement.* Mahwah, NJ: Lawrence Erlbaum.

Cooke, N. J., Salas, E., Cannon-Bowers, J. A., & Stout, R. J. (2000). Measuring team knowledge. *Human Factors, 42,* 151-173.

Crego, J., & Spinks, T. (1997). Critical incident management simulation. In R. Flin, E. Salas, M. Strub, & L. Martin (Eds.), *Decision making under stress* (pp. 85–94). Aldershot, UK: Ashgate.

Dake, K. (1992). Myths of nature and the public. *Journal of Social Issues, 48,* 21–38.

Department of Homeland Security. (2003) *Top Officials (TOPOFF) Exercise Series: TOPOFF 2. After action summary report.* Washington, DC: Author.

Dunning, C. (2003). Sense of coherence in managing trauma workers. In D. Paton, J. M. Violanti, & L. M. Smith (Eds.), *Promoting capabilities to manage posttraumatic stress: Perspectives on resilience* (pp. 119–135). Springfield, IL: Charles C Thomas.

Endsley, M., & Garland, D. (2000) *Situation awareness: Analysis and measurement.* Mahwah, NJ: Lawrence Erlbaum.

Entin, E. E., & Serfaty, D. (1999). Adaptive team coordination. *Human Factors, 41,* 312–325.

Federal Emergency Management Agency. (2004). *Responding to incidents of national consequence.* Washington, DC: Author.

Flin, R. (1996). *Sitting in the hot seat: Leaders and teams for critical incident management.* Chichester, UK: Wiley.

Flin, R., & Arbuthnot, K. (2002) *Incident command: Tales from the hot seat.* Ashgate, UK: Aldershot.

Flin, R., Salas, E., Strub, M., & Martin, L. (Eds.). (1997). *Decision making under stress.* Aldershot, UK: Ashgate.

Gist, R., & Woodall, J. (2000). There are no simple solutions to complex problems. In J. M. Violanti, D. Paton, & C. Dunning (Eds.), *Posttraumatic stress intervention: Challenges, issues and perspectives* (pp. 81–96). Springfield, IL: Charles C Thomas.

Grant, N. K., Hoover, D. A., Scarisbrick-Hauser, A., & Muffet, S. L. (2003). The crash of United Flight 93 in Shanksville, Pennsylvania. In J. L. Monday (Ed.), *Beyond September 11: An account of post disaster research* (Special Publication No. 39). Boulder: Natural Hazards Research & Applications Information Centre, University of Colorado.

Gunderson, L. H., Holling, C. S., & Light, S. (1995). *Barriers and bridges to the renewal of ecosystems and institutions.* New York: Columbia University Press.

Hart, P. M., & Wearing, A. J. (1995). Occupational stress and well-being: A systematic approach to research, policy and practice. In P. Cotton (Ed.), *Psychological health in the workplace.* Carlton: Australian Psychological Society.

Higgins, G. O. (1994). *Resilient adults: Overcoming a cruel past.* San Francisco: Jossey-Bass.

Hood, C., & Jones, D. K. C. (1996). *Accident and design: Contemporary debates in risk management.* London: UCL Press.

Huddleston, L., Paton, D., & Stephens, C. (In press). Conceptualizing traumatic stress in police officers: Preemployment, critical incident and organizational influences. *Traumatology.*

Jackson, B. A., Baker, J. C., Ridgely, M. S., Bartis, J. T., & Linn, H. I. (2003). *Protecting emergency responders volume 3: Safety management in disasters and terrorism response.* Cincinatti, OH: National Institute for Occupational Safety and Health.

Janoff-Bulman, R. (1992). *Shattered assumptions.* New York: Free Press.

Johnston, P., & Paton, D. (2003). Environmental resilience: Psychological empowerment in high-risk professions. In D. Paton, J. Violanti, & L. Smith (Eds.), *Promoting capabilities to manage post-traumatic stress: Perspectives on resilience* (pp. 136–151). Springfield, IL: Charles C Thomas.

Kendra, J., & Wachtendorf, T. (2003). Creativity in emergency response to the World Trade Center disaster. In J. L. Monday (Ed.), *Beyond September 11: An account of post disaster research* (Special Publication No. 39). Boulder: Institute of Behavioral Science, Natural Hazards Research and Applications Information Centre, University of Colorado.

Linley, P. A., & Joseph, S. (2004). Positive change following trauma and adversity: A review. *Journal of Traumatic Stress, 17,* 11–21.

Lyons, R. F., Mickelson, K. D., Sullivan, M. J. L., & Coyne, J. C. (1998). Coping as a communal process. *Journal of Social and Personal Relationships, 15,* 579–605.

MacLeod, M. D., & Paton, D. (1999). Police officers and violent crime: Social psychological perspectives on impact and recovery. In J. M. Violanti & D. Paton (Eds.), *Police trauma: Psychological aftermath of civilian combat.* Springfield, IL: Charles C Thomas.

Mitroff, I. I., & Anagnos, G. (2001). *Managing crises before they happen.* New York: Amacom.

Moran, C., & Colless, E. (1995). Positive reactions following emergency and disaster responses. *Disaster Prevention and Management, 4,* 55–61.

Moran, C. C. (1999). Recruits' prediction of positive reactions in disaster and emergency work. *Disaster Prevention and Management, 8,* 177–183.

Park, C. L. (1998). Stress-related growth and thriving through coping: The roles of personality and cognitive processes. *Journal of Social Issues, 54,* 267–277.

Paton, D. (1994). Disaster relief work: An assessment of training effectiveness. *Journal of Traumatic Stress, 7,* 275–288.

Paton, D. (1997). *Dealing with traumatic incidents in the workplace* (3rd ed.). Queensland, Australia: Gull.

Paton, D., & Flin, R. (1999). Disaster stress: An emergency management perspective. *Disaster Prevention and Management, 8,* 261–267.

Paton, D., & Jackson, D. (2002). Developing disaster management capability: An assessment centre approach, *Disaster Prevention and Management, 11,* 115–122.

Paton, D., Johnston, D., Houghton, B., Flin, R., Ronan, K., & Scott, B. (1999). Managing natural hazard consequences: Information management and decision making. *Journal of the American Society of Professional Emergency Managers, 6,* 37–48.

Paton, D., & Stephens, C. (1996). Training and support for emergency responders. In D. Paton, & J. Violanti (Eds.), *Traumatic stress in critical occupations: Recognition, consequences and treatment.* Springfield, IL: Charles C Thomas.

Paton, D., & Violanti, J. M. (2006). Terrorism stress risk assessment and management. In B. Bongar, L. Beutler, P. Zimbardo, L. Brown, & J. Breckenridge (Eds.), *Psychology of terrorism* (pp. 225–246). New York: Oxford University Press.

Paton, D., Violanti, J. M., & Smith, L. M. (2003). *Promoting capabilities to manage posttraumatic stress: Perspectives on resilience.* Springfield, IL: Charles C Thomas.

Paton, D., & Wilson, F. (2001). Managerial perceptions of competition in knitwear producers. *Journal of Managerial Psychology, 16,* 289–300.

Raphael, B. (1986). *When disaster strikes.* London: Hutchinson.

Scotti, J. R., Beach, B. K., Northrop, L. M. E., Rode, C. A., & Forsyth, J. P. (1995). The psychological impact of accidental injury. In J. R. Freedy & S. E. Hobfoll (Eds.), *Traumatic stress: From theory to practice.* New York: Plenum.

Shakespeare-Finch, J., Paton, D., & Violanti, J. (2003). The family: Resilience resource and resilience needs. In D. Paton, J. Violanti, & L. Smith (Eds.), *Promoting capabilities to manage posttraumatic stress: Perspectives on resilience* (pp. 170–185). Springfield, IL: Charles C Thomas.

Solomon, S. D., & Smith, E. S. (1994). Social support and perceived control as moderators of responses to dioxin and flood exposure. In R. J. Ursano, B. G. McCaughey, & S. Fullerton (Eds.), *Individual and community responses to trauma and disaster* (pp. 197–200). Cambridge, UK: Cambridge University Press.

Stout, R. J., Cannon-Bowers, J. A., Salas, E., & Milanovich, D. M. (1999). Planning, shared mental models and coordinated performance: An empirical link is established. *Human Factors, 41,* 61–71.

Tedeschi, R. G., & Calhoun, L. G. (2003). Routes to posttraumatic growth through cognitive processing. In D. Paton, J. M. Violanti, & L. M. Smith (Eds.), *Promoting capabilities to manage posttraumatic stress: Perspectives on resilience* (pp. 12–26). Springfield, IL: Charles C Thomas.

Thompson, J. (1993). Psychological impact of body recovery duties. *Journal of the Royal Society of Medicine, 86,* 628–629.

Tugade, M. M., & Frederickson, B. L. (2004). Resilient individuals use positive emotions to bounce back from negative emotional experiences. *Journal of Personality and Social Psychology, 86,* 320–333.

Violanti, J. M., & Paton, D. (2006). *Who gets PTSD? Issues of vulnerability to posttraumatic stress.* Springfield, IL: Charles C Thomas.

Weick, K. E. (1995). *Sensemaking in organizations.* Thousand Oaks, CA: Sage.

Williams, T. (1993). Trauma in the workplace. In J. P. Wilson & B. Raphael (Eds.), *International handbook of traumatic stress syndromes* (pp. 925–934). New York: Plenum.

Current Best Practices
Coping with Major Critical Incidents

DONALD C. SHEEHAN, GEORGE S. EVERLY,
JR., AND ALAN LANGLIEB

The combined tragedies of September 11, 2001, have merged into a significant American generational marker not experienced since the assassination of President John F. Kennedy. Nowhere have the cascading consequences of these watershed events impacted more than on the law enforcement profession. Critical incidents are a recognized part of the law enforcement experience. After all, it is a high-risk profession. Normally, critical incidents occur on a small scale, affect only a few people, and cause only short-term burdens on existing organizational resources. The events related to September 11th, however, clearly deviated from the norm. Protecting human resources within law enforcement always has been a challenge, but critical incidents, such as those experienced on September 11th, pose extraordinary difficulties requiring extreme responses. From such adversities invariably come innovations, lessons learned, and, ultimately, even greater response capabilities.

Reviewing the evolving practices of uniquely experienced organizations, commonly referred to as an analysis of best practices, can prove informative. Therefore, the authors have undertaken such an analysis of some of America's uniquely experienced law enforcement organizations regarding their ongoing efforts to assist their personnel in coping with critical incidents, both small and large scale. As the first survey of its kind, this may represent a significant contribution to the profession.

Background

The practice of providing critical incident stress management and support services to law enforcement personnel has a rich history, but the origins of such assistance actually can be traced to the military. Wars and conflicts have punctuated this country's history since its inception.

Technological advances in weaponry beginning with the Civil War produced causalities of a type and scale previously not experienced by medical personnel. Out of sheer necessity in the face of incredible, large-scale suffering, they had to add newly constructed intervention principles to traditional treatment practices. In time, the recognition of the importance of immediate intervention led to the assimilation of corpsmen and medics into combat units. During the Korean Conflict the military moved medical units forward to gain proximity to the battlefields. Hard-won experience produced expectancy about the types of injuries that medical personnel could treat successfully. By the time the armed forces were engaged in Vietnam, their medical units had instituted triage as a standard practice that systematically assigned a priority to the treatment of the wounded based on such factors as urgent need, the chance of survival, and the amount of resources available.

What affects the mind affects the body, and what affects the body affects the mind.[1] The two are inextricably intertwined and cannot be separated. The shell shock of World War 1 and the combat fatigue of World War II proved just as potentially debilitating to soldiers as many of their physical wounds. The military discovered that the principles established for treating physical traumas also applied to treating psychological ones. "Nothing could be more striking than the comparison between the cases treated near the front and those treated far behind the lines….

As soon as treatment near the front became possible, symptoms disappeared… with the result that 60 percent with a diagnosis of psychoneurosis were returned to duty from the field hospital. War neuroses… could be controlled by scientific management, rather than allowing nature to take its course."[2] "Those on field duty found it to be most advantageous to the soldier, and to the army, to recognize exhaustion and the tear but not to remove the soldier to the rear…. By and large, the prognosis… varies directly with the time factor… the great issue … is not to permit the syndrome to become entrenched … the most effective implement is to keep alive the [causal] relation between the symptoms and the traumatic event.'"

These military observations became concretized as the three pillars of crisis intervention: proximity (the ability to provide psychological support wherever needed in the field), immediacy (the ability to provide rapid support), and expectancy (viewing adverse reactions to critical incidents as basically normal reactions of extreme stress and not as pathological reactions). The three became known collectively as the P.I.E. Principle[4] and formed the historical foundation of crisis intervention not only for the military but also for law enforcement. The type of trauma experienced by soldiers in combat is quite similar to that endured by law enforcement officers. In short, the law enforcement profession adopted the best practices of the military.

Method

The application of best practices can be a highly effective way to deal with complex problems. Law enforcement professionals do not have the luxury of sitting back and theorizing when confronted with catastrophes. They usually have to act immediately to establish public order in the wake of the disorder caused by large-scale critical incidents. Practical, logistical, and time constraints make it difficult to conduct the randomized controlled trial, which is the gold standard researchers use to compare the effectiveness of intervention. Therefore, copying the successful tactics of other agencies that have dealt with similar problems becomes an effective and efficient strategy. It saves valuable time and resources at the most critical point, the immediate aftermath of an incident.

In recognition of this concept, Dr. Everly initiated a survey in the spring of 2003 to ascertain what various law enforcement agencies and organizations have done to support their personnel during extraordinary critical incidents. Sadly, New York, New Jersey, Washington, DC, and Pennsylvania were not the only locations affected by mass crisis. The jarring horror of losing so many children in Waco, Texas, and Oklahoma City, Oklahoma, stand as equally traumatic events. Regardless of geographic location or size, all law enforcement agencies face potential, large-scale incidents.

Survey Participants

The authors included 11 organizations based on accrued unique experience responding to the psychological demands associated with extraordinary critical incidents and mass disasters. They consulted federal, state, and city organizations to provide a balanced perspective for dealing with catastrophic events and obtained information from interviews with program directors and from written descriptions. Many of these programs not only are innovative but represent prime exemplars of a structured response to the unique psychological needs of those in the law enforcement profession.

BUREAU OF ALCOHOL, TOBACCO, FIREARMS, AND EXPLOSIVES

The Bureau of Alcohol, Tobacco, Firearms, and Explosives (ATF) initiated its Peer Support/ Critical Incident Stress Management Program in 1989 out of concern for special agents involved in shootings and other critical incidents. Administered via the Office of the Ombudsman, a program manager, who is a mental health clinician, provides clinical oversight. The ATF program serves all 6,000 employees and their families, as well as stale and local law enforcement partners who represent 25 to 30 percent of the program workload.

The ATF Peer Support Program has four components: peer responders, mental health professionals, chaplains, and trainers. The 43 peer support personnel are not counselors but special agents, inspectors, and other key personnel with over 60 hours of specialized training. Mental health providers make referrals to the agency's employee assistance personnel or to community resources as necessary. Sixty chaplains provide spiritual support and critical incident stress management interventions. ATF professional development personnel conduct related training.

ATF uses a comprehensive, multicomponent critical incident stress management model that includes preincident education, assessment of need and management consultations, individual peer support, large-group crisis intervention, family support services, small-group crisis intervention, chaplain or pastoral care services, referral and follow up, and debrief-the-debriefer sessions. Based on the specifics of a particular incident. ATF has tailored its intervention plan to reach and accommodate those directly or indirectly impacted by a critical incident.

COP 2 COP

Cop 2 Cop serves 40,000 law enforcement officers, plus family members, in the New Jersey Port Authority Police, New York State Police, and the New Jersey Urban Search and Rescue Unit. Established in 1998, it became fully operational on November I, 2000, through the use of a widely circulated, toll-free telephone number (1-866-COP-2COP). The staff consists of 4 retired clinicians with experience treating law enforcement officers, 4 mental health specialists, and 48 retired law enforcement officers who voluntarily answer the telephone hotline.

Following the terrorist attacks. Cop 2 Cop's role expanded to include all New Jersey firefighters and emergency medical service personnel. The program also provided intervention services to Secret Service and FBI agents residing in New Jersey. In the aftermath of September 11th, the program initiated acute traumatic stress leadership training and implemented a unique large-group "reentry program."

Cop 2 Cop employs an integrated, multicomponent emergency mental health continuum-of-care approach, including telephone hotlines, one-on-one crisis intervention, telephone assessments, group crisis intervention, and referrals to mental health resources.

Since its inception, the program has received over 9,000 telephone calls and has conducted more than 450 critical incident stress management interventions.

FBI

The FBI uses a two-pronged approach in delivering stress management services to approximately 28,000 employees and their families. The FBI Academy emphasizes training and research. It teaches stress management; examines stress-related issues, such as domestic violence and suicide,[5] in televised forums and publications; and is developing an early warning tool tor detecting excessive stress reactions by law enforcement officers.[6]

The FBI's Employee Assistance Unit, consisting of several mental health professionals and support personnel, became self-contained in 1993. It coordinates delivery of four primary services and represents an integrated, multicomponent continuum-of-care model, including preincident training, assessment, triage, individual crisis intervention, small-group crisis intervention, psycho-educational seminars, family support services, and chaplain referrals. Specifically, 300 coordinators, positioned throughout the organization, provide assessment, short-term counseling, and referrals to employees experiencing a wide range of problems. Critical incident stress management—a peer-based, small-group crisis intervention—occurs subsequent to exposure to critical incidents. Peer support/post-critical incident seminars (residential group psycho-educational interventions) follow significant critical incidents, such as shootings and mass disasters. These last up to 4 days and began in 1983 in response to agent-involved shooting incidents. Over 100 experienced volunteer chaplains provide pastoral counseling, family support, death/bereavement services, and individual or small-group crisis intervention.

FEDERAL LAW ENFORCEMENT TRAINING CENTER

The Office of Critical Incident Stress Management, Federal Law Enforcement Training Center (FLETC), Department of Homeland Security supports 40,000 students from approximately 76 federal law enforcement agencies each year. It also serves permanent and detailed staff, participating organizational personnel, employees, contractors, visitors, and their families.

FLETC formally established its Critical Incident Stress Management and Peer Support Program in 1999. Eight teams, comprised of 50 employees, provide services throughout the United States and abroad.

The center integrates a multidisciplinary standard-of-care continuum with specific services, including precrisis education/inoculation; individual, team, mental health practice, and community basic and advanced training; triage/assessment/referral for initial/follow-up treatment; individual peer support; small- or large-group defusing; small-group debriefing or demobilization; individual traumatic stress reduction management; pastoral/bereavement counseling; employee assistance services; and a wellness program.

NATIONAL FRATERNAL ORDER OF POLICE

The National Fraternal Order of Police (FOP) originally established its Critical Incident Committee in 1996. But, in 2001, it reformulated this entity as the Critical Incident Stress Management Program to provide affected emergency service workers with services that mitigated or lessened the impact of the effects of critical incident stress and accelerated the recovery following a traumatic event. FOP designed the program to prevent or mitigate the adverse psychological reactions that so often accompany emergency services, public safety, and disaster response functions. Interventions in this program are directed toward the mitigation of post-traumatic stress reactions. Fundamental to the FOP approach is a philosophy and a belief in the importance and value of the human response, especially within the occupation of law enforcement.

Key services include consultation to local law enforcement, critical incident education programs, development of a national law' enforcement emergency response strike team to assist wherever needed, and the establishment of a central repository for available law enforcement critical incident stress management programs nationwide. FOP uses an integrated, multicomponent crisis intervention system that includes precrisis education seminars, individual crisis intervention services, group crisis interventions, demobilizations, defusings, debriefings, chaplain services, family interventions, organizational consultation, follow-up resources, and referral to formal mental health services as indicated.

NEW JERSEY ATTORNEY GENERAL'S OFFICE AND STATE POLICE

Established in 2003, New Jersey's Critical Incident Stress Response Program functions within a preexisting employee assistance program. In addition to traditional services, it sponsors a unique command staff leadership series that covers ethics-based leadership, law enforcement family dynamics, terrorism, and psychological counterterrorism. The New Jersey model offers an integrated, multicomponent crisis intervention system with a full spectrum of employee assistance services.

NEW YORK CITY: POLICE ORGANIZATION PROVIDING PEER ASSISTANCE

In 1994 and 1995, the 26 police officer suicides generated grave concerns throughout New York City. In response to this alarming phenomenon, the city created the Police Organization Providing Peer Assistance (POPPA), an autonomous, independent, confidential, and voluntary police assistance agency. Volunteer peer support personnel received training in crisis intervention and critical incident stress management and began staffing a 24-hour hotline in March 1996.

Currently, POPPA has an administrative staff consisting of a director, clinical director, peer liaison, consulting staff, and a case manager; a clinical panel of over 120 psychologists, psychiatrists, social workers, and addictions counselors trained and motivated to work with police officers; and 180 peer support officers. Available at all times, these individuals meet with distressed officers in neutral, private locations. They provide referrals only at face-to-face meetings. All meetings, referrals, and subsequent treatment remain strictly confidential. Since 1996, over 6,500 face-to-face meetings have taken place.

POPPA uses an integrated, multicomponent critical incident stress management intervention system adapted to best meet the needs of law enforcement personnel and the unique demands of each specific critical incident. It operates on the basis of a self-referral system. POPPA key interventions include assessment, triage, individual crisis intervention, demobilizations (large-group crisis intervention), defusings (small-group crisis intervention), debriefings (small-group format), and referral to subsequent psychological support if required.

OKLAHOMA CITY: CRITICAL INCIDENT WORKSHOPS

The April 19, 1995. terrorist bombing in Oklahoma City precipitated a series of critical incident workshops. Estimates indicated that 20 percent of the 12,384 rescue personnel involved would require some form of mental health care. As of October 2002, over 750 rescue personnel, survivors, volunteers, and family members have received direct service from 70 workshops, which use an intensive 4-day format. Intervention teams consist of a facilitator, psychologist, chaplain, and a trained crisis intervention peer support individual.

Workshops use key interventions, such as individual crisis intervention, small-group critical incident stress debriefing, family support, education, chaplain/pastoral services, referrals, and follow-up care. The workshops offer eye movement desensitization and reprocessing (EMDR), a highly controversial but effective technique, as an optional treatment.

U.S. MARSHALS SERVICE

In 1991, the U.S. Marshals Service (USMS) initiated its Critical Incident Response Team (CIRT). Staffed by 3 mental health professionals and 51 peer support personnel, CIRT extends services to over 4,200 employees and their family members. Incident-specific response teams consist of an employee assistance representative and one or two peer support marshals. USMS uses an integrated, multicomponent intervention continuum-of- care approach consisting of assessment, triage, individual crisis intervention, small-group crisis intervention (defusings and debriefings), large-group crisis intervention, organizational development, family intervention services, and referral to psychotherapeutic resources.

U.S. SECRET SERVICE

The U.S. Secret Service (USSS) implemented its Critical Incident Peer Support Team in 1985. Administered from its Employee Assistance Program (EAP), the peer support team has expanded to include agents, uniformed officers, and administrative support staff. It includes 4

EAP counselors and 86 peer support personnel, who receive specialized training in crisis intervention and critical incident debriefings. Designated peer support counselors assist EAP counselors with precrisis education seminars for new agents and uniformed officers. Field intervention teams consist of an EAP counselor and one or two peer support personnel. USSS uses an integrated, multicomponent intervention approach consisting of assessment, triage, individual crisis intervention, small-group debriefings, precrisis education seminars, family intervention services, follow-up resources, and referral to mental health professionals as needed.

WORLD TRADE CENTER—RESCUER SUPPORT VICTIM PROGRAM

Because first responders comprised approximately 400 of the 2,800 victims of the September 11th disasters, this program began in 2002 to serve law enforcement, firefighters, and emergency medical personnel. It has three primary components: 1) crisis intervention hotline help, 2) crisis intervention training programs, and 3) clinical intervention services. On a pro bono basis, the program provides peer counseling, individual crisis intervention, and individual therapy and uses a structured, six-session, group treatment model.

The program's main purpose is to give voice to the rescuers. The conceptual framework includes partnership with management, establishment of funding, consultation of nationally recognized experts, collaboration with clinicians, use of peer support, and reliance on logistical and planning flexibility.

Key Findings

Five best practices emerged from the many practical, empirically field-tested strategies used to deal with large-scale critical incidents. They almost are universal, and agencies should consider them in any organizational approach to effective critical incident stress management.

EARLY INTERVENTION

The survey revealed that the law enforcement agencies sampled recognized the value of early psychological intervention for those officers responding to critical incidents. This echoed earlier military experience regarding the importance of immediate intervention in treating physical and psychological wounds.

COMPLETE CARE

All of the organizations sampled recommended the use of a phase-sensitive, multicomponent crisis intervention system as part of an overall continuum of care. Such a system underscores the necessity of employing strategic planning prior to implementation.

PEER SUPPORT

Each participant emphasized the importance of peer support and saw it as a virtual imperative to a successful law enforcement program. Consistent with this tactical formulation, not one of the organizations viewed crisis intervention as psychotherapy nor as a substitute for it.

SPECIALIZED TRAINING

All of the organizations acknowledged the importance of receiving specialized training in crisis intervention/emergency mental health (for both peer interventionists, as well as mental health clinicians) prior to implementing such programs. Well-meaning intentions are not enough. Officers exposed to traumatic events need focused assistance by trained practitioners at all levels of care, ranging from hotline assistance to therapeutic treatment.

TACTICAL INTERVENTION

Tactical interventions, in most programs, included the ability to perform one-on-one small- and large-group crisis interventions and family support services, as well as the ability to access spiritual support assistance and treatment resources. The word *tactical* refers to adroit maneuvering used to achieve a desired objective. The military connotation is highly appropriate in any discussion of psychological trauma induced by critical incidents. Much of the psychological assistance given to public safety and emergency personnel in the domestic terrorism of Oklahoma City and in the international terrorism of New York City was based on lessons learned during conventional wars.

Core Competencies

Five core competencies appeared as features of a best practices model. These elements offer law enforcement agencies an effective way to help their personnel deal with critical incidents.

ASSESSMENT AND TRIAGE

Agencies need to rapidly evaluate affected officers and provide them with assistance consistent with the resources at hand. Integral to the process of assessment, however, is knowing when *not* to interfere with natural coping mechanisms. Simply said, law enforcement often can be a stressful profession, but formal crisis intervention always should yield to the individual's natural coping mechanisms and resources as long as these function effectively.

CRISIS INTERVENTION WITH INDIVIDUALS

Officers differ in their responses, and their agencies must remember that mass critical incident care is not a one-size-fits-all proposition. Crisis intervention skills applied to one individual at a time (face- to-face or telephonically) represent the bedrock of all emergency mental health techniques and always begin with the assessment of their suitability.

SMALL-GROUP CRISIS INTERVENTION

Peers supporting each other in a group setting can be highly effective and efficient. The small-group crisis intervention format (e.g., debriefings) can be a useful intervention mechanism.[7] Care must be taken, however, to ensure that vicarious traumatization does not occur. This is best achieved by using homogeneous functional groups of individuals who have experienced the same level of psychological toxicity via their exposure. Similarly, care must be taken so as not lo encourage excessive ventilation, coercive group pressure, or scapegoating (targeting individuals or organizational policy).

LARGE-GROUP CRISIS INTERVENTION

A town meeting provides another way for people to process the tumultuous events engulfing them. Typically employed with large groups, this type of crisis intervention is largely a psycho-educational process designed to enhance cohesion, control rumors, improve self-assessment, and make individuals aware of coping techniques and resources.[8] Agencies may apply this method many different ways, including in the format of roll call.

STRATEGIC PLANNING

"The process is strategic because it involves preparing the best way to respond to the circumstances of the organization's environment, whether or not its circumstances are known in advance.... The process is about planning because it involves intentionally setting goals... and developing an approach to achieving those goals."[9] Thus, strategic planning allows operational planners to best combine and sequence multiple interventions within an integrated Incident Command System. All strategic planning, as well as tactical intervention, must be predicated upon ongoing assessment.

Future Directions

Large-scale critical incidents spring from all manner of causes. Some result from upheaval and disruption of the natural order. The air, earth, fire, and water that normally sustain people become the hurricanes, earthquakes, wildfires, and floods that destroy them. Other major critical incidents result from human activity, such as war and terrorism. Both types of critical incidents impact everyone. No group is more affected than those who impose order upon the chaos resulting from major critical incidents. In response to the acute mental health needs of those in crisis, the field of crisis intervention was born.

The majority of law enforcement officers exposed to a traumatic event will not need formal psychological intervention, but that does not negate the obligation to respond to the needs of those who will require acute psychological support. Information regarding critical incidents, common reactions, and sources of support could benefit everyone.

An observation about firefighters applies equally well to law enforcement officers. "In all the controversy, criticism, and research debate on the merits of debriefing [i.e., early psychological intervention], certain constants are emerging. The most effective methods for mitigating the effects of exposure to trauma... those, which will help keep our people healthy and in service, are those, which use early intervention, are multimodal and multi-component. That is, they use different 'active ingredients'... and these components are used at the appropriate time with the right target group."[10]

Most of the emphasis of existing programs is on managing the reactions to mass critical incidents after they occur. This direct approach, while practical and goal oriented, does not encompass the full range of options available. The key to optimizing existing programs is to focus on preincident strategies.

PREINCIDENT TRAINING

The study of the current and historical military response to psychological trauma has become quite useful in developing an effective and efficient law enforcement model for mass critical incident stress management. For example, a British military psychiatrist and his colleagues found that debriefing techniques even reduced alcohol use after stressful assignments.[11]

However, one lesson remains from the military that the law enforcement profession has not sufficiently incorporated into its programs, the principle of expectancy. Two Israeli psychologists investigated roles of immediacy, proximity, and expectancy.[12] Results indicated that all three early intervention principles contributed to therapeutic outcome, with expectancy supplying the most to positive outcome. As earlier research noted, to a significant degree, the soldier's expectation of outcome predicted recovery from war neurosis.[13] The military experience demonstrated that the law enforcement profession must do a better job of managing the expectations of officers to ensure their psychological well-being after a major critical incident.

To illustrate the apparent importance of expectation management for new and experienced law enforcement professionals, the authors present some real-life examples. Approximately every 2 weeks, 50 agent trainees arrive at the FBI Academy on a Sunday afternoon. On the following Wednesday morning, they are issued the handguns they will carry throughout their law enforcement careers. For 5 years, on the afternoon after they received their weapons, Special Agent Sheehan taught the trainees a block of instruction called Stress Management in Law Enforcement. He always started the 7-hour course by asking how many of them would be surprised if they actually had to use their service weapon. Virtually everyone said it would be a surprise. He then would point out some hard facts. First, while at the academy, they will fire thousands of rounds until they can quickly and accurately fire 50 rounds at targets 25 to 5 yards away. Next, they must qualify with a minimum score of 80 percent four times a year during their employment. Also, every day that they are on duty for those 20 to 30 years, they will have to carry their weapon. In addition, every year, the FBI holds critical incident seminars, and many agents who are shooters or shootees attend. Following a shooting, approximately 79 percent of involved officers have reported time distortion and 52 percent have indicated memory loss for part of the

event.[14] And, finally, estimates have indicated that the career of a law enforcement officer is shortened significantly after a shooting incident. Under these circumstances, new employees need to change their expectations about what could happen to them.

This change in expectations is necessary for the more experienced members of the law enforcement community as well. Several years ago, Special Agent Sheehan went to Belfast, Northern Ireland, at the request of the Royal Irish Constabulary to address the Association of Chief Police Officers of England, Scotland, Wales, and Northern Ireland about violence in the United States. He asked these experienced and highly accomplished officers what shocked them the most about the events that had occurred at Columbine High School in Colorado. Their answers ranged from gun violence to sudden death. They were partially right, of course, but, in the authors' view, the aspect that ultimately bothers most people about that event was the brutal violation of what their expectation of the school experience should be. Children should be able to go to school in safety without the fear of immediate death.

Everyone has expectations. Sometimes, these get violated. In the law enforcement profession, expectations can be destroyed in an abrupt and massive way. In an era of incipient terrorism, agencies must provide proactive training. In 2003, the Institute of Medicine stated, "The committee finds that terrorism and the threat of terrorism will have psychological consequences for a major portion of the population, not merely a small minority.... The stress associated with the direct impact and lingering threat of terrorism raises obvious psychological concerns, particularly for... first responders...."[15]

Conducting more preincident education offers the best way to change expectations. Some training is taking place, but not enough. For example, although the FBI provides agent trainees with some preincident training, it offers no such regularly scheduled training for journeymen agents in the field. Even flu vaccines are administered on a yearly basis. Critical incident education provides one of the best inoculations available to law enforcement officers facing toxic situations. If they expect something, they are better able to cope with it. The military has firmly established that expectation management saves lives. Universally, the law enforcement community must do a more thorough job of creating realistic expectations through preincident training.

EARLY WARNING SCREENING

People differ in their responses to critical incidents. Some officers adjust rapidly, whereas others adapt gradually. A small number adjust poorly and develop an extreme reaction called post-traumatic stress disorder (PTSD). A 2002 study revealed that 13 percent of rescue personnel developed PTSD,[16] a significantly higher rate than the 1 to 3 percent in the general population. This suggested that rescue workers, like law enforcement officers, face elevated risk due to increased exposure to traumatic events. According to the military principle of immediacy, these people need to be identified early. Immediate identification of acute problems allows for the mobilization of higher-ordered interventions, which work best *before* problems become habitual and fully assimilated.[17] Training peers and managers to recognize the first signs of maladaptive responses must occur. When managing critical incident stress, law enforcement agencies need to remember that the sooner they intervene, the better.

Conclusion

A number of occupations are at high risk for psychological distress and morbidity. Law enforcement constitutes one such profession. The corpses of fellow citizens, the ruins of buildings, and the wreckage of all types of conveyances scorch the senses and poison the memories of law enforcement officers. If society exposes them to these harsh aspects of life, it is morally bound to give them the best possible psychological support. Current state-of-the-art early psychological intervention programs within the law enforcement profession emphasize post-incident intervention. Expansion of early intervention services to include precrisis expectation training and early warning screening could move existing programs to the cutting edge of mass critical incident management. No agency has created a perfect model, but a number of organizations have developed workable programs for dealing with acutely stressful events. Regardless of the size of the department, the men and women who have dedicated themselves to protecting their communities will benefit from adopting these best practices.

The authors offer a special thanks to the survey contributors who made this article possible. Law enforcement officers in their respective organizations benefit from the daily efforts of these dedicated professionals. Now, because of their willingness to share such hard-won experience, all law enforcement officers and their supporters can benefit as well.

ENDNOTES

1. G. S. Everly, Jr and J. M. Lating, *A Clinical Guide to the Treatment of the Human Stress Response* (New York, NY: Kluwer/Plenum, 2002); and D.C Sheehan. "Stress Management in the Federal Bureau of Investigation: Principles tor Program Development," *international Journal of Emergency Mental Health* 1 (1999): 39–42.

2. T. S. Salmon, "War Neuroses and Their Lesson," *New York Medical Journal* 108 (1919): 993–994.

3. A. Kardnier, "The Traumatic Neuroses of War," *Psychosomatic Medicine Monographs* 11 (1941): 11–111.

4. K, Artiss, "Human Behavior Under Stress: From Combat to Social Psychiatry," *Military Medicine* 128 (1963): 1011–1015.

5. D.C. Sheehan, ed., U.S. Department of Justice, Federal Bureau of Investigation, *Domestic Violence by Police Officers* (Washington, DC, 2000); and D.C. Sheehan and J.J. Warren, eds., U.S. Department of Justice, Federal Bureau of Investigation, *Suicide and Law Enforcement* (Washington, DC, 2001).

6. For additional information, see D.C. Sheehan and V.B. Van Hasselt, "Identifying Law Enforcement Stress Reactions Early," *FBI Law Enforcement Bulletin,* September 2003, 12–17.

7. M. Arendt and E. Elklit, "Effectiveness of Psychological Debriefing," *Acta Psychiatrica Scandinavica* 104 (2001): 423–437: A Dyregrov, "Psychological Debriefing: An Effective Method?" *Traumatoloy* vol. 4, issue 2 (1998), see http://www.fsu.edu/~trauma; and M. Deahl, M. Srinivasan, N. Jones, J. Thomas, C. Neblett, and A. Jolly, "Preventing Psychological Trauma in Soldiers: The Role of Operational Stress Training and Psychological Debriefing." *British Journal of Medical Psychology* 73 (2000): 77–85.

8. G.S. Everly, Jr., "Crisis Management Briefings," *International Journal of Emergency Mental Health* 2 (2000): 53–57.

9. What Is Strategic Planning?"; retrieved on April 6, 2004, from *http://www.nonprofits.org/apofaq/03/22. html.*

10. H. Duggan, International Association of Fire Chiefs, "CISM at the World Trade Center: Lessons Learned," *IAFC On Scene,* January 2002; retrieved on April 7, 2004, from http://www.iafc.org.

11. M. Deahl. M. Srinivasan, N. Jones, J. Thomas, C. Neblett, and A. Jolly, "Preventing Psychological Trauma in Soldiers: The Role of Operational Stress Training and Psychological Debriefing," *British Journal of Medical Psychology* 73 (2000): 77–85.

12. Z. Solomon and Z. and R. Benbenishty, "The Role of Proximity, Immediacy, and Expectancy in Frontline Treatment of Combat Stress Reaction Among Israelis in the Lebanon War." *American Journal of Psychiatry* 143 (1986): 613–617.

13. Supra note 3.

14. A. Artwohl, "Perceptual and Memory Distortion During Officer-Involved Shootings," *FBI Law Enforcement Bulletin,* October 2002, 18–24.

15. Institute of Medicine, *Preparing for the Psychological Consequences of Terrorism* (Washington, DC: National Academies Press, 2003).

16. C. S. North, L. Tivis, et al., "Psychiatric Disorders in Rescue Workers After the Oklahoma City Bombing," *American Journal of Psychiatry* 159 (2002): 857–859.

17. The Law Enforcement Officer Stress Survey identified areas officers find most troubling; supra note 6.

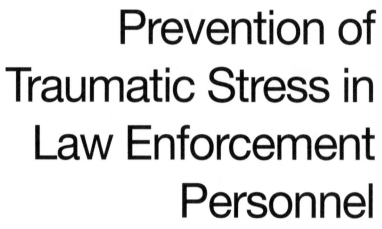

Prevention of Traumatic Stress in Law Enforcement Personnel

A Cursory Look at the Roles of Peer Support and Critical Incident Stress Management

RICHARD L. LEVENSON JR., PSYD, CTS

Abstract

Law enforcement is considered to be one of the most stressful careers. Constant exposure to horrific scenes of death, tragedy, and human suffering may result in debilitating and, ultimately, life-threatening psychological illnesses. Because law enforcement communities are typically resistant to outside interventions, training mental-health paraprofessionals (peer support officers) to work with police officers has been a successful alternative. By using critical incident stress management (CISM), a technique of emotional first aid, peer-support officers can achieve results equal to, or better than, many mental-health professionals.

This article outlines the seven-stage model of CISM, a comprehensive, integrated, and multi-component continuum approach to crisis intervention.

Law enforcement ranks as one of the most stressful careers. Yet, traditionally, law enforcement officers (LEOs) dealing with significant and debilitating job-related stress have avoided reaching out for help, especially within their own departments. These officers fear being labeled *troubled* and are concerned that they will be seen as ineffective, unable to undertake normal work responsibilities, unworthy of promotion, and unable to carry firearms. The fact that LEOs think they must maintain image-armor further exacerbates their stress levels and is another obstacle to obtaining help.

In terms of the costs of *not* seeking help, Mitchell states, "for many law enforcement personnel, the results of severe or prolonged stress can be seen in poor job performance, disrupted relationships, declining health, changes in personality, the development of Post Traumatic Stress Disorder (PTSD) and, in extreme cases, even suicides" (p. 215). Another factor playing into the decision not to seek help is a mistrust of the mental health profession—a fear that the disclosure of how the LEO feels will be used against him or her and adversely impact his or her career.

Despite assurances of confidentiality, most LEOs remain suspicious and mistrustful of the mental-health professionals who are there to help the officers return to pre-crisis levels of functioning. The failure to address critical incidents and stressful events, sometimes over the course of their entire professional careers, creates a cumulative effect that places many LEOs at risk for stress-related disorders (e.g., poor mental health, alcohol and substance abuse, cardiologic, vascular, and gastrointestinal illnesses). Internalizing both traumatic scenes they have witnessed and life-threatening situations in which they have been involved settles into a foundation that cannot support healthy functioning. As a result, the LEO's energy is invested in holding him or herself together in order to make it through each day.

Law enforcement communities typically are resistant to outside interventions, so training mental-health paraprofessionals has been one successful way of treating stress-affected LEOs. The use of paraprofessionals in many fields has been well-established for over 40 years (Carkhuff & Truax, 1965; Durlak, 1979). In law enforcement, these paraprofessionals are called peer support officers (PSOs) (Levenson & Dwyer, 2003). These active-duty (and sometimes retired) LEOs around the country serve on their own departmental teams and are on call to provide "mental-health critical care" (Levenson, 2005) to officers who reach out to their fellow specially-trained officers. According to George S. Everly, PSOs are specifically trained in crisis intervention assessment and techniques and are under the supervision of a licensed clinician (as cited in Levenson & Dwyer). Research has shown that paraprofessionals "frequently achieve clinical outcomes equal to or better than those obtained by professionals" (Levenson & Dwyer, p. 148). Appropriately training paraprofessionals is essential; the use of standardized treatments (Durlak), a careful and meticulous selection procedure (Sheehan, 1999), all-encompassing primary training (Hattie, Sharpley, & Rogers, 1984), and ongoing supervision from licensed mental health professionals and more experienced PSOs (Clifford, 1999) are all key elements in PSO training.

Having PSOs conduct preliminary assessments and provide peer-counseling support to LEOs serves a number of functions. First, LEOs are comfortable speaking to peers who know the job intimately and, thus, understand their traumatic experiences. The issues of suspiciousness and mistrust with respect to confidentiality are virtually non-existent. LEOs who are seen as needing more intensive clinical intervention and support are more likely to accept a referral to an outside-the-department mental-health professional who has been identified through prior screening as having had specialized training working with members of the law enforcement community.

Peer support officers are an interesting group, and the mixture of law enforcement knowledge with an interest in, and acceptance of, the mental health profession makes for a more fully functioning department. There is little doubt that the support PSOs provide helps reduce sick days and job-related disability claims, keeps families intact, and lowers the rate of officers' suicides. After noting the positive effects on personnel, some departments have made regular debriefings mandatory, as providing emotional support and stress management is important in these highly emotionally charged environments. The beneficial effects of peer counseling have been shown in numerous research investigations with federal agents (Sheehan, 1999) and police officers (Chamberlin, 2000; Freeman, 2002; Greenstone, 2000).

The Role of Critical Incident Stress Management

Human reactions to man-made disasters (i.e., terrorism) are more psychologically debilitating than reactions to natural disasters, such as earthquakes, floods, and hurricanes. It seems likely that terrorism is more stressful psychologically due to its unpredictability in terms of occurrence and scope of destruction. According to Everly and Mitchell (1999), a psychological crisis results from feelings of distress associated with a critical incident. In a psychological crisis, there is a marked stress increase, where coping mechanisms stop working, and there is "evidence of significant distress, impairment, and dysfunction" (p. 10). The goal of crisis intervention techniques is to stabilize the individual by reducing symptoms and facilitating return to pre-crisis levels of functioning or to provide access to more specialized mental-health critical care.

Critical incident stress management (CISM) is now in world-wide use by many law enforcement organizations as well as emergency services, hospitals, schools, business, industrial, and banking institutions. CISM is also a service that is funded—or reimbursed—by men- tal-health insurance policies and plans of most major health insurance companies. In concurrence with earlier definitions developed by Mitchell (1983; 1996), Everly and Mitchell (1999) denote CISM as a "comprehensive, integrated, multi-component continuum approach to crisis intervention" (p. 15). CISM is designed to mitigate the severe psychological distress brought on by involvement in some traumatic event or situation, and techniques associated with CISM also may serve to reduce the impact of PTSD should it evolve. CISM is part of a multi-faceted program of crisis intervention techniques, which include, but are not limited to, both one-on-one and group debriefings. A rich cascade

Table 6.1. Elements of CISM (Everly & Mitchell, 2003)

- Pre-incident education, preparation
- Demobilizations (large groups of public safety)
- Crisis Management Briefings (large groups of primary, secondary emergency personnel, and tertiary–family, co-workers, etc., and victims)
- Defusings (small groups)
- Critical Incident Stress Debriefing (CISD) (small groups)
- One-on-one crisis intervention
- Family CISM
- Organizational/Community Intervention, consultation
- Pastoral crisis intervention
- Follow-up and referral for continued care

Note. Table reproduced by permission of the International Critical Incident Stress Foundation, Inc.

of services, beginning at pre-incident training and ending with post-incident response, is available (See Table 6.1). Despite a controversy initiated by Bisson, McFarland, and Rose (2000) suggesting that debriefings were neither efficacious nor helpful (Everly & Mitchell, 2003), empirically sound research has provided strong support for short-term, CISM group and individual services to a wide variety of populations (e.g., Boscarino, Adams, & Figley, 2005; Everly & Piacentini, 1999). CISM is considered to be emotional first-aid and is *not* psychotherapy, nor are psychotherapeutic services part of the CISM continuum. The CISM team is peer-driven, but a CISM-trained mental-health professional is a member in order to provide supervision and support, as well as specific educational information during a debriefing.

Critical Incident Stress Debriefing (CISD) for adults is a seven-phase process, consisting of *Introduction, Fact, Thoughts, Reactions, Symptoms, Teaching,* and *Re-Entry.* A debriefing is neither a critique nor an investigation (Mitchell, 2001), and the phases are led by a PSO, with the exception of the *Teaching Phase,* which is conducted by a mental-health professional who is a regular member on CISM teams.

During the *Introduction Phase,* the team is introduced, a brief explanation and rationale are given, and confidentiality is assured as notes or recordings are *not* made, nor are officers' ranks considered. In the *Fact Phase,* participants are asked about themselves, their roles in or exposure to the event, and their perspectives. In the *Thought Phase,* first impressions or prominent thoughts are elicited. During the *Reactions Phase,* participants are encouraged to share their emotional responses including what they viewed as the most disturbing or worst part of the event. In the *Symptoms Phase,* the goal is to acknowledge any bodily changes noted on scene, both during and later (such symptoms might be increased heart rate, upset stomache, headache, nausea, and others too numerous to mention). The *Teaching Phase* is vital to help those involved realize that they have experienced normal feelings during and after an abnormal event, which serves to help normalize the entire experience for the LEO. In that regard, the need for re-establishing normal routines, which includes the individual's usual amount of sleep, exercise, food, self-care, and talks with trusted friends, is stressed. Expectations and any concerns are also discussed in this phase. Lastly, there is the *Re-Entry Phase,* during which questions may be asked and are answered, the CISD is summarized and any loose ends are tied up, and participants are reminded about confidentiality. If the mental-health professional believes that one or more of the participants might benefit from a referral for personal counseling services, that discussion occurs after the CISD is concluded. Typically, PSOs and trained mental-health professionals who work together in CISM agree on which LEO-CISD participants need more intensive clinical services.

It is not the role of CISM teams in law enforcement to cure those with whom they interact. No single team can alleviate all symptoms or return every single individual to healthy functioning, as each person reacts to stressful events in different ways. As Mitchell (1996) states, "CISM teams work to mitigate the impact of the event and to accelerate the recovery of personnel from traumatic stress reactions" (p. 217).

Conclusion

There is great need for quality stress management programs in law enforcement, and perhaps the most important aspect of any program is an endorsement by a director, chief, or other administrative commander. Therefore, LEOs should be able to see that their superiors acknowledge their repeated exposure to job-related stressors and provide LEOs with a climate of acceptance. The situations in which LEOs are involved can severely impact common and healthy people and lead to "normal (but painful) reactions to abnormal or unusual circumstances" (Mitchell, 1996, p. 216). Because officers exposed to traumatic events need to be aware of the types of psychological reactions one might experience as a result of involvement in domestic terrorism, mass disaster, or horrific crime scenes, pre-incident training is one of the most crucial aspects of any law enforcement critical incident response team.

References

Bisson, J. I., McFarlane, A., & Rose, S. (2000). Psychological debriefing. In E. Foa, A. McFarlane, & M. Friedman (Eds.), *Effective treatments for PTSD* (pp. 39–59). New York: Guilford.

Boscarino, J. A., Adams, R. E., & Figley, C. R. (2005). A prospective cohort study of the effectiveness of employer-sponsored crisis interventions after a major disaster. *International Journal of Emergency Mental Health, 7*(1), 9–22.

Carkhuff, R. R., & Truax, C. B. (1965). Lay mental health counseling: The effects of lay group counseling. *Journal of Consulting Psychology, 29*(5), 426–431.

Chamberlain, J. (2000). Cops trust cops, even one with a Ph.D. *APA Monitor, 31,* 1.

Clifford, B. (1999). The New South Wales Fire Brigades' critical incident stress management response to the Thredbo landslide. *International Journal of Emergency Mental Health, 1*(2), 127–133.

Durlak, J. A. (1979). Comparative effectiveness of paraprofessional and professional helpers. *Psychological Bulletin, 86*(1), 80–92.

Everly, G. S., Jr., & Mitchell, J. T. (1999). *Critical incident stress management (CISM): A new era and standard of care in crisis intervention* (2nd Ed.). Ellicott City, MD: Chevron Publishing Co.

Everly, G. S., Jr., & Mitchell, J. T. (2003). *Critical incident stress management CISM: Individual crisis intervention and peer support.* Ellicott City, MD: International Critical Incident Stress Foundation, Inc.

Everly, G. S., Jr., & Piacentini, A. (1999, March). *The effects of CISD on trauma symptoms: A meta-analysis.* Paper presented at the APA-NIOSH Work, Stress and Health '99: Organization of Work in a Global Economy Conference, Baltimore, MD.

Freeman, G. (2002). 9/11 one year later, ACFE members reflect: What have we learned? *The Forensic Examiner, 11*(9-10), 10–15.

Greenstone, J. L. (2000). Peer support in a municipal police department. *The Forensic Examiner, 9*(3–4), 33–36.

Hattie, J. A., Sharpley, C. F., & Rogers, H. J. (1984). Comparative effectiveness of professional and nonprofessional helpers. *Psychological Bulletin, 95*(3), 534–541.

Levenson, R. L., Jr. (2005). On the cutting edge of mental health critical care. *International Journal of Emergency Mental Health, 7*(1), 59.

Levenson, R. L., Jr., & Dwyer, L. A. (2003). Peer support in law enforcement: Past, present, and future. *International Journal of Emergency Mental Health, 5*(3), 147–152.

Mitchell, J. T. (1983). When disaster strikes… The critical incident stress debriefing process. *Journal of Emergency Medical Services, 8*(1), 36–39.

Mitchell, J. T. (1996). Systematic approach to critical incident stress management in law enforcement organizations. In J. T. Reese, & R. M. Solomon (Eds.), *Organizational Issues.* Washington, DC: U. S. Department of Justice, Federal Bureau of Investigation.

Mitchell, J. T. (2001). *QuickCards.* Ellicott City, MD: Chevron Publishing Co.

Sheehan, D. C. (1999). Stress management in the Federal Bureau of Investigation: Principles for program development. *International Journal of Emergency Mental Health, 1*(1), 39–42.

The FBI's Critical Incident Stress Management Program

VINCENT J. MCNALLY AND ROGER M. SOLOMON, Ph.D.

L ine-of-duty shootings; death, suicide, or serious injury of co-workers; multi-casualty homicides; and hostage situations exemplify critical incidents that often leave law enforcement officers feeling an over-whelming sense of vulnerability or lack of control.[1] The FBI recognizes that two-thirds of officers involved in shooting incidents may experience significant emotional reactions. Typical responses include a heightened sense of danger; flashbacks and nightmares; intrusive imagery and thoughts; anger; guilt; sleep

Vincent J. McNally and Roger M. Solomon, "The FBI's Critical Incident Stress Management Program," *FBI Law Enforcement Bulletin*, vol. 68, no. 2, pp. 20-26. U.S. Department of Justice, 1999. Copyright in the Public Domain.

difficulties; withdrawal; depression; and stress symptoms. These represent *normal reactions to abnormal situations.*

In the 1970s, when little was known about critical incident trauma, about 70 percent of police officers who used fatal force left law enforcement within 5 years.[2] Even today, the failure to resolve issues associated with critical incidents often leads to a variety of negative cognitive and behavioral patterns. Some law enforcement officers may overreact to perceived threats; others may underreact to clearly dangerous situations. Some officers resign or retire prematurely, while others become disciplinary problems or develop increased absenteeism. Burnout, stress-related illnesses, posttraumatic stress disorder, and substance abuse often result from unresolved issues stemming from traumatic incidents.

Critical Incident Interventions

The FBI has a responsibility to help its employees constructively handle the emotional aftermath of critical incidents. Accordingly, the Employee Assistance Unit developed the Critical Incident Stress Management (CISM) Program to safeguard and promote the psychological well-being of FBI employees following traumatic experiences. While agents always have received training, firearms, and body armor to help them physically survive critical incidents, they now can obtain the tools they need to help them survive the emotional aftermath of such events.

The CISM Program provides FBI employees with a confidential method of mitigating the adverse effects of the incidents and promoting positive resolution. Team members are drawn from the Employee Assistance Unit, FBI chaplains, the FBI peer support team, and mental health professionals with expertise in police psychology and trauma. Although ail CISM team members do not have legally sanctioned privileged communication, interventions are considered confidential by policy. Moreover, all FBI team members receive training on the importance of maintaining confidentiality and supporting their fellow employees without judging or losing respect for them.

The program offers a continuum of interventions and services, which provides both immediate and long-term support. These include defusings, critical incident stress debriefings, family outreach, manager support, referrals and follow-up services, eye movement desensitization and reprocessing treatments, and postcritical incident seminars.

DEFUSINGS

After initial investigative issues (e.g., conducting preliminary interviews and taking statements) have been handled, the CISM team will convene a defusing.[3] This informal small group or individual discussion with involved personnel begins a few hours after the incident. These 30- to 40-minute interventions promote normalization, reduce tension, and determine future needs.

CRITICAL INCIDENT STRESS DEBRIEFINGS

After the initial defusing occurs, the next level of intervention involves a critical incident stress debriefing (CISD),[4] a structured group discussion for all involved personnel that takes place as the emotional impact sets in. Depending on personnel needs, logistical considerations, and legal issues (e.g., waiting until investigative statements have been taken), the CISD usually occurs within 24 to 72 hours after the incident.

The CISD promotes normalization and recovery by having involved personnel discuss such issues as their roles in the incidents, their thoughts during the events, their emotional reactions, and the stress symptoms they experienced. In addition to educating these employees about coping strategies, the CISD enables CISM team members to determine who may benefit from referrals for further care and to plan for other follow-up support.

PEER OR ONE-ON-ONE SUPPORT

Following the debriefing, the CISM team may meet individually with the employees involved in the incident. Often, a team member who has experienced a similar critical incident will provide the one-on-one support. Peer guidance proves particularly effective in helping FBI personnel normalize their reactions to the trauma. This support has tremendous credibility coming from a fellow employee who has "been there."

FAMILY ASSISTANCE

In the law enforcement profession, an employee's most vital support system, the family, often remains neglected. Individuals adversely affected by critical incidents bring the trauma home to their families.[5] The CISM team provides debriefings for family members as a group and one-on-one to help them cope with their reactions to a family member's involvement in a critical incident.

MANAGER SUPPORT

The CISM team consults with managers about their roles in supportively handling the emotional aftermath of critical incidents. Managers must coordinate communication, timetables for crisis services, appropriate ongoing interventions, and other support programs. FBI experience has shown that recovery occurs more rapidly when concerned managers actively nurture their employees following a traumatic event. Moreover, additional traumatic stress may result when employees perceive managers as distant or insensitive.

Additionally, managers must remember that critical incidents, especially those involving death or serious injury to coworkers, can significantly impact the entire office. Appropriate and timely intervention by both managers and the CISM team can minimize the negative consequences for office personnel and others affected by the incident.

REFERRALS AND FOLLOW-UP SERVICES

For many individuals, defusings, debriefings, and one-on-one support lead to closure and resolution of the traumatic incident. Through this assistance, the traumatic incident is processed and becomes integrated; specifically, negative emotions, thoughts, and images fade. The individual retains what is useful, learns from the incident, and resolves the event.

However, for others, these interventions represent only a beginning. The intense physiological and psychological arousal of a critical incident can impair their information-processing mechanisms. Consequently, information taken in during the trauma (e.g., sights, sounds, emotions, sensations, and beliefs) can be "frozen" in the brain and not processed normally.[6] Rather than fading, these sensory impressions can continue to intrude, resulting in flashbacks, nightmares, intrusive thoughts, and other posttraumatic symptoms.[7] A central component of the trauma can be negative, irrational self-beliefs having to do with an individual's participation in the event (e.g., "It's all my fault... I'm still not safe... I'm helpless"). At this point, referral to mental health professionals with specialized experience and training becomes necessary.

EYE MOVEMENT DESENSITIZATION AND REPROCESSING

Eye movement desensitization and reprocessing (EMDR) is a component of the FBI's integrated response to critical incidents. A therapeutic method that must be administered only by mental health professionals trained in the procedure, EMDR frequently accelerates the treatment of trauma. Reportedly, EMDR stimulates the brain's natural information-processing mechanisms, allowing the "frozen" traumatic information to be processed normally

Examples of Line-of-Duty Critical Incidents

- » Experiencing the death or violent traumatic injury of a co-worker, spouse, or family member

- » Taking a life, or causing serious injury, in a line-of-duty situation

- » Experiencing the suicide of a co-worker, spouse, or family member

- » Surviving a major natural disaster or man-made catastrophe (e.g., bombing)

- » Witnessing/handling multiple fatalities

- » Participating in high-speed pursuit that ends in tragedy

- » Participating in Special Weapons and Tactics (SWAT) operations, where dangers are present

- » Negotiating with a hostage taking/barricaded suspect

- » Observing an act of corruption, bribery, or other illegal activity by a co-worker

- » Facing suspension and/or threat of dismissal

and achieve integration.[8] Negative images often fade; negative emotions subside. Irrational thoughts give way to appropriate, adaptive thoughts and interpretations (e.g., "I did the best I could...I survived and I am now safe...I can exercise control"). With EMDR, an individual discards what is not useful (e.g., irrational thoughts, distressing emotions, intrusive images), retains what is useful, and learns from the event, as the following hypothetical example illustrates.

A male rescue worker at the bombing of the Federal Building in Oklahoma City felt guilty over not finding some missing limbs of one victim. He felt he had not completed his mission. Also, he felt guilty that it had taken several days to recover another victim that had been visible but inaccessible. He experienced intrusive images of the scenes, which evoked significant distress. Given debriefings and counseling, the worker still experienced intrusive images and feelings of guilt. Two months after the incident, he received EMDR. During treatment, the worker realized that no one had ever found the missing limbs and that he had done all he could. Applying EMDR to the second situation involving the delayed recovery, the worker realized that the victim was dead, not calling for help, and that the rescuers had other priorities. He then stated that not only had he done the best he could but that he and his fellow rescuers had done a good job. His guilt was alleviated.

Research indicates that after three 90-minute sessions of EMDR, 84 to 100 percent of individuals who had posttraumatic stress disorder (PTSD) due to a single traumatic episode no longer met the criteria for PTSD.[9] Consistent with this research, the FBI has found EMDR to be effective when used with individuals exhibiting symptoms of posttraumatic stress stemming from a specific event.

Most important, only mental health professionals should administer EMDR. While critical incident stress debriefings and defusings illustrate crisis intervention strategies, EMDR constitutes treatment, which requires education and skill to administer. Therefore, mental health professionals must have appropriate training in EMDR, as well as knowledge and experience in working with trauma.

POSTCRITICAL INCIDENT SEMINAR

Critical incident recovery can prove a lengthy and complex process. Even after initial acceptance and resolution of an incident, negative reactions can resurface. Once individuals confront their vulnerability and mortality, they must learn to live with that reality. Going through a traumatic incident is like crossing a road and losing one's naivete with no possibility of crossing back.[10] To minimize longterm difficulties, the CISM team members and employee assistance personnel make follow-up contacts. Also, they offer referrals for additional help as needed.

To promote resolution and provide follow-up support, the FBI initiated a postcritical incident seminar (PCIS). Employee assistance staff members invite employees who have experienced a critical incident to a 4-day seminar to discuss their reactions in a safe, protective, and confidential environment. Also open to the spouses of employees involved in traumatic events, the seminar usually includes between 15 and 25 individuals. Through sharing their experiences with others, participants receive peer support, which helps normalize their reactions. They also learn about trauma and coping strategies to facilitate healing and recovery. Additionally, peer support training permits participants to offer constructive interpersonal support in the future to fellow employees who may experience critical incidents.

The PCIS allows participants experiencing difficulty to access professional services in a safe environment. Participants can work voluntarily one-on-one with clinicians who specialize in law enforcement issues, posttraumatic stress disorder, and EMDR. Often the vehicle that moves individuals who are "stuck" in resolving their incidents, PCIS can be illustrated by the following example.

While attending a PCIS, an agent experienced distress from a seemingly minor incident.[11] During the surveillance of a suspected drug dealer, a high-speed chase ensued. The suspect, realizing he was being followed, drove at speeds in excess of 100 miles per hour. He eventually pulled over, got out of his vehicle, and approached the agent. The agent identified himself, and the suspect surrendered upon command.

Despite the positive outcome, the incident still bothered the agent. At the PCIS, the agent talked about this incident and realized his fear stemmed from the accumulation of several past incidents. These included Vietnam experiences, two air disasters, and several hostage negotiations. The agent recognized the connection between the surveillance and these other situations where he faced his own mortality. With EMDR, further discussion, and peer support, the agent resolved these cumulative stress issues. Over the past 2 years, follow-up contact has revealed that these gains remain stable.

The PCIS commonly deals with issues of vulnerability resulting from such situations as the trauma of witnessing a partner's being shot, grief stemming from the sudden death of a loved one, guilt from having to use fatal force, or the horror that comes from working with mass casualties following a bombing or airline disaster.

Since 1986, the FBI has conducted 37 of these seminars with 900 participants. Many of those who have attended a PCIS volunteer to assist others who experience critical incidents. Valuable resources because they have experienced such incidents, these employees and spouses provide enlightened interpersonal support to their peers following traumatic events. The FBI believes that no better individuals exist to offer support than those who have experienced, and emotionally worked through, similar events.

THE ONE-TWO PUNCH

The combination of eye movement desensitization and reprocessing with the postcritical incident seminar has led to rapid recovery in FBI employees experiencing posttraumatic stress from singleepisode trauma. Although EMDR generally proves effective in one to three 90-minute sessions, the FBI's experience shows that the therapeutic gains occur even more rapidly when EMDR is used within the context of the PCIS.

Though EMDR does not work for everyone, the FBI's experience with single-episode trauma reveals that a 30- to 40-minute session results in a significant reduction of posttraumatic reactions. The safe atmosphere, peer debriefing, and educational information initiate a positive working-through process, which prepares the employee for further intervention using EMDR.

Similarly, employing EMDR soon after a critical incident stress debriefing or a one-on-one session, as a "one-two punch," has been found to be helpful for personnel suffering from single-episode trauma who have a stable support system.[12] The CISD or one-on-one structure facilitates an understanding of the impact of the event and provides support and guidance toward adaptive resolution.

EMDR appears to have a very powerful and rapid effect after such intervention, perhaps because of this initial processing. Not a one-time therapy procedure, several EMDR sessions may be needed to resolve the incident. Therefore, follow-up contact remains essential.

Most important, EMDR following a CISD or one-on-one session, or used within the context of a postcritical incident seminar works best for individuals experiencing acute symptoms from a specific incident who have stable support systems and living situations. Though EMDR is applicable for complex posttraumatic stress reactions or symptoms due to cumulative stress, a more thorough preparation and assessment should be completed before initiating EMDR. Further, because EMDR sometimes can open up other emotional issues and stimulate unresolved traumas, it should be administered by a trained clinician who can determine the appropriateness of the therapy. Follow-up contact proves essential to ensure treatment effects remain stable and to deal with other emotional issues that may arise.

This one-two punch has led to an enhanced role for peer support personnel by increasing their interaction with mental health professionals. Under the supervision of a clinician, peers often help prepare employees for the EMDR session by discussing the impact of the incident, debriefing employees following the treatment, and providing follow-up contact.

Peers report a greater sense of satisfaction because of their closer involvement in the healing process. Clinicians appreciate the peer assistance because the initial preparation can save time. The close working relationship between clinicians and peers has led to earlier intervention than conventional referral can afford, which ultimately benefits the affected employee.

Conclusion

The FBI's Critical Incident Stress Management Program offers a continuum of integrated confidential services beginning immediately following an incident and extending to long-term, follow-up support. Along with immediate interventions (e.g., defusings, critical incident stress debriefings, peer support, and referrals), the CISM program provides long-term, follow-up contact through the post- critical incident seminar. Also, eye movement desensitization and reprocessing, a therapeutic method for the treatment of trauma, is an integrated component of the FBI's response to a traumatic incident. Whether assisting employees in coping with the emotional aftermath of such events as the bombing of the Federal Building in Oklahoma City or the TWA Flight 800 crash in New York, the FBI has demonstrated its commitment to a comprehensive approach to critical incident stress programs.

These intervention methods may prove helpful to other law enforcement agencies faced with similar situations. The safeguarding of law enforcement personnel cannot stop at providing officers with only the weapons and equipment to fight crime but must include giving these brave men and women the strategies for coping with the emotional aftermath of traumatic events that occur all too frequently in their profession.

Endnotes

1. R.M. Solomon, "Critical Incident Stress Debriefing in Law Enforcement," in *Innovations in Disaster and Trauma Psychology,* ed. G.S. Everly and J.T. Mitchell (Ellicott City, MD: Chevron Publishing, 1995), 123–157.

2. James M. Horn, "Critical Incidents for Law Enforcement Officers," in *Critical Incidents in Policing,* eds. James T. Reese, James M. Horn, and Christine Dunning (Washington, DC: Government Printing Office, 1991), 143.

3. J.T. Mitchell and G.S. Everly, *Critical Incident Stress Debriefing: An Operations Manual for the Prevention of Traumatic Stress Among Emergency Services and Disaster Workers,* 2d ed., rev. (Ellicott City, MD: Chevron Press, 1996).

4. Ibid.

5. G.S. Everly, "Familial Psychotraumatology in Emergency Services Personnel," in *Innovation in Disaster and Trauma Psychology,* vol. 2, ed. G.S. Everly and J.T. Mitchell, (Ellicott City, MD: Chevron Publishing. 1995), 42-50.

6. F. Shapiro, *Eye Movement Desensitization and Reprocessing: Principles, Protocols and Procedures* (New York: Guilford, 1995).

7. R.M. Solomon and J.S. Horn, "Postshooting Traumatic Reactions: A Pilot Study," in *Psychological Services in Law Enforcement,* ed. J. Reese and H. Goldstein (Washington DC: Government Printing Office, 1986), 383–393.

8. Supra note 5; see also F. Shapiro and R.M. Forrest, *Eye Movement Desensitization and Reprocessing: The Breakthrough Therapy* (New York: Basic Books, 1997); F. Shapiro and R.M. Solomon, "Eye Movement Desensitization and Reprocessing: Neurocognitive Information Processing," in *Innovations in Disaster and Trauma Psychology,* ed. G.S. Everly (Ellicott City, MD: Chevron Publishing, 1995), 216–237; R. M. Solomon and F. Shapiro, "Eye Movement Desensitization and Reprocessing: An Effective Therapeutic Tool for Trauma and Grief," in *Death and Trauma,* ed. C. Figley, B. Bride, and M. Nicholas (Washington, DC: Taylor and Francis, 1997), 231–248.

9. B.O. Rothbaum, "A Controlled Study of Eye Movement Desensitization and Reprocessing in the Treatment of Posttraumatic Stress Disordered Sexual Assault Victims," *Bulletin of the Menninger Clinic* 61 (1997), 317–334; S.A. Wilson, L.A. Becker, and R.H. Tinker, "Eye Movement Desensitization and Reprocessing (EMDR) Treatment for Psychologically Traumatized Individuals," *Journal of Counseling and Clinical Psychology* 63 (1995): 928–937; S. Marcus, P. Margris, and C. Sakai, "Controlled Study of Treatment for EMDR in an HMO Setting," *Psychotherapy* 34 (1997): 307-315; S.A. Wilson,

L.A. Becker, and R.H. Tinker, "Fifteen-Month Follow-up of Eye Movement Desensitization and Reprocessing (EMDR) Treatment for PTSD and Psychological Trauma," *Journal of Counseling and Clinical Psychology,* in press; M.M. Scheck, J.A. Schaeffer, and C.S. Gillette, "Brief Psychological Intervention with Traumatized Young Women: The Efficacy of Eye Movement Desensitization and Reprocessing," *Journal of Traumatic Stress,* in press.

10. Supra note 1.

11. Permission granted by the FBI agent to disclose this example.

12. J.T. Mitchell and R.M. Solomon, *CISM and EMDR,* paper presented at the Fourth World Congress on Stress. Trauma, and Coping in the Emergency Services Professions, Baltimore, MD, April 5, 1997.

CPSIA information can be obtained
at www.ICGtesting.com
Printed in the USA
BVHW061248220722
642605BV00004B/278